A SURVIVAL GUIDE FOR LIFE

How to achieve your
goals, thrive in adversity
and grow in character

BEAR GRYLLS

CORGI BOOKS

TRANSWORLD PUBLISHERS
61–63 Uxbridge Road, London W5 5SA
A Random House Group Company
www.transworldbooks.co.uk

A SURVIVAL GUIDE FOR LIFE
A CORGI BOOK: 9780552168625

First published in Great Britain
in 2012 by Bantam Press
an imprint of Transworld Publishers
Corgi edition published 2013

Copyright © Bear Grylls Ventures 2012

Bear Grylls has asserted his right under the Copyright, Designs and Patents Act 1988
to be identified as the author of this work.

'Gone to the Edge' by Christopher Logue, copyright © Christopher Logue, 1996 and
printed with permission of Faber and Faber Ltd.

A CIP catalogue record for this book
is available from the British Library.

Addresses for Random House Group Ltd companies outside the UK
can be found at: www.randomhouse.co.uk
The Random House Group Ltd Reg. No. 954009

The Random House Group Limited supports the Forest Stewardship Council®
(FSC®), the leading international forest-certification organisation. Our books
carrying the FSC label are printed on FSC®-certified paper. FSC is the only
forest-certification scheme supported by the leading environmental organisations,
including Greenpeace. Our paper procurement policy can be found at
www.randomhouse.co.uk/environment

Design by Julia Lloyd
Printed and bound by CPI Group (UK) Ltd, Croydon, CR0 4YY.

6 8 10 9 7

This book is written for our three boys: Jesse, Marmaduke and Huckleberry.

Sometimes life can be tough, but I hope this can serve as a good route map to guide you through the challenges and on towards your dreams. Life is short and precious – live it boldly, my special ones.

We love you so much and are so proud of you. For ever.

Thank you, my beautiful Shara, for being my rock, my friend and my encouragement. I like to think that together we make a pretty solid team...

I have come that they may have life, and have it to the full.

JOHN 10:10

CONTENTS

A SURVIVAL GUIDE FOR LIFE

1.
HAVE A DREAM

This isn't a get-rich-quick book – this is an insider's guide on how to follow your heart, and live an empowered, effective, fun-filled life. And in a contest between the two, there is only ever one real winner.

The place to start this life journey is with finding your dream.

Dreams are powerful. They are among those precious few intangibles that have inspired men and women to get up, go to hell and back, and change the world.

And I'm not talking about the sort of fantasy dreams that can't physically happen – I am talking about the sort of dream that will inspire you, one that you are really prepared to sweat for, in order to make it become your reality.

This quote from T. E. Lawrence means a lot to me:

All men dream; but not equally. Those who dream by night in the dusty recesses of their minds wake in the day to find that it was vanity: but the dreamers of the day are dangerous men, for they may act their dreams with open eyes, to make it possible.

Our job is to be the dangerous type. The one who dreams by day and acts to make those dreams come alive and actually happen.

So take some time to get this right. Go for a long walk. Think big. Think about what really makes you smile.

Ask yourself what you would do if you didn't need the money. Ask yourself what really excites you. Ask what would inspire you to keep going long after most people would quit.

Find those answers and therein lies your dream. We all have our own personal Everest, and if we follow its calling, that is when life truly becomes an adventure.

Obviously your dream needs to be realistic and achievable, so use your common sense and exercise good judgement – but don't confuse realism with pessimism! Think big, make sure it is physically possible, and as long as the key ingredients to achieving it are vision and hard work, then go for it.

Now, many might say: 'I don't need to have goals to be successful.' But they would be wrong.

In life, it is hard enough to reach your peak when you know where you want to go; but it is near impossible to reach those heights if you don't even know where the mountain range is!

In order to grow, you must have a dream and you must have a clear goal.

Write it down. Pin it on your wall – somewhere you will see it every day.

Words and pictures have power.

Got it?

OK, we have begun…

2.
DON'T LISTEN TO THE DREAM-STEALERS

The very next thing that will happen, once you write your goals down and start to talk to people about them, is that you will meet those all-too-common cynics who will look at you and smirk.

I call them the dream-stealers.

Beware: they are more dangerous to mankind than you might ever imagine.

In life, we will never be short of people who want to knock our confidence or mock our ambitions.

There are lots of reasons why people might want to rain on your parade: perhaps they're a little jealous that you want more out of life than they might hope for, or they're worried your success will make them feel inferior. It might be that their motives come from a better place and they just want to spare you the failure, heartache and tears.

Either way, the results are the same: you get dissuaded from achieving your dreams and from fulfilling your potential.

The key is not to listen to them too hard. Hear them, if you must – out of respect – but then smile and push on.

Remember, the key to your future success is going to be embracing the very same things those dream-stealers are warning you about: the failure, the heartache and the tears.

All those things will be key stepping stones on the road to success, and are actually good solid markers that you are doing something right.

3.
JUST
BEGIN...

The greatest journeys all start with a single step.

When you stand at the bottom of a mountain, you can rarely see a clear route to the top. It is too far away and the path too twisty and hidden behind obstacles. **The only way to climb the sucker is to start – and then keep putting one foot in front of the other, one step at a time.**

There's a quote from Martin Luther King that I love:

Take the first step in faith. You don't have to see the whole staircase. Just take the first step.

It is good advice.

When you are setting out on a long and difficult journey towards your goal, you will not be able to foresee every obstacle or anticipate every lucky break. But what you will find is that with every step you gain experience, perspective, skill and confidence. It is these elements that will ultimately help you reach your goal.

But you only gain experience, perspective, skill and confidence when you start moving.

See how it works now?

Sometimes the journey ahead can feel so daunting and so implausible that we lack the courage to take the first step. And there is never a shortage of good excuses: it's not the right time; the odds are too stacked against me; or no one like me has ever done it before.

I'm also willing to bet that Neil Armstrong, the first man on the moon, Sir Edmund Hillary, the first man to climb Everest, or even Thomas Edison, trying thousands and thousands of times to make the light bulb work, had a good list of excuses that they could have used, too.

And I can promise you they all felt inadequate at many times along their path.

You know what the sad thing is? It's that most people never find out what they are truly capable of, because the mountain looks frightening from the bottom, before you begin. It is easier to look down than up.

There's a poignant poem by Christopher Logue that I'm often reminded of when people tell me their 'reasons' for not embarking on a great adventure.

Come to the edge.

We might fall.

Come to the edge.

It's too high!

COME TO THE EDGE!

And they came,

And we pushed,

And they flew.

I have a sneaking suspicion that if you can just take that first step off the edge, you might find that you, too, can fly.

If you can just take that first step towards your own dreams – take that enormous leap of faith towards beginning whatever it is – then new possibilities open up before you.

It is the magic of beginning. Things start to happen.

Then it is all about hanging on for the ride – keeping cheerful, not quitting, trusting the right people, listening to that inner voice, doing what others won't or can't, and never losing sight of the goal.

But more of all that good stuff to come…

4.
CHASE THE GOAL, NOT THE MONEY

We live in a society where people love to equate success with money. It is always a mistake.

I have met enough unhappy millionaires to know that money alone does not make you happy. I've seen people work so hard they do not have any time for their families (or even time to enjoy the money).

They doubt their friends' motives, or become paranoid about people trying to steal from them.

Wealthy people can all too easily end up feeling guilty and unworthy, and it can be a heavy load to carry – especially if you don't treat that fickle impostor right.

You see, money, for its own sake, like success or failure, is a thing of little lasting significance. It is what we 'do' with it and how we treat it that makes the life-changing difference.

Money, success and failure can drastically improve or ruin people's lives. So you have got to treat it for what it is. And you have got to stay the master of it.

Wealthy people so often find that the summit of their mountains – the success that they sought – isn't enough. And they are right. It isn't enough to satisfy our deep hunger for meaning and purpose. (And we will talk about that later on.)

In essence, you have got to build your house on good foundations – on rock, not sand – and money as a goal in itself will never satisfy you.

So choose wisely. And be careful what you wish for. When you start putting the correct steps into place, good things will start to happen. So you have got to be prepared for the success when it comes.

Money can make the path more comfortable, but it will never remove the potholes.

The billionaire John Paul Getty famously said: 'I would give everything I own for one happy marriage.' That is pretty telling. Money doesn't solve all your ills. **In fact, money, like success, tends, instead, to magnify your life – and if you are living with the wrong values, money will make things much worse.**

Conversely, if you get it right, money can be an incredible blessing.

So always keep referring back to page 15 at the start of this book. Look at your dream. Never lose sight of it, because if you attain it, you will be rich beyond measure…and I'm not talking dollars and cents.

A final note on this, one little secret: when you truly commit yourself to your dream, when you ooze enthusiasm and let your talents shine (however small or fledgling they might be at the start), you will often find that the money comes to you by default. But if you just chase the money, like a butterfly, it will often fly away.

Follow the dream and let your talent thrive, better people's lives, stick to it through thick and thin, and I bet you find out that money will be close beside you.

So try not to worry about money, ever – instead focus on the journey. And certainly don't waste time and energy accumulating just wealth.

Follow your goals wholeheartedly and there will be enough to satisfy you.

Just wait and see where your dreams can take you.

5.
BE THE MOST ENTHUSIASTIC PERSON YOU KNOW

My mum and dad gave me a few bits of great advice as a young boy (along with a fair amount of scolding for being an idiot, but that's another story!), but there is one thing my late father told me that has affected my outlook and approach to life more than almost anything else, and it was this:

If you can be the most enthusiastic person you know, then you won't go far wrong.

It was always said to me with a wry smile, as if I was being told something of infinite power. And he was right.

Enthusiasm so often makes the critical difference: it sustains you when times are tough, it encourages those around you, it is totally infectious and it rapidly becomes a habit!

In turn, that enthusiasm adds the extra 5 per cent sparkle to everything we do – and life is so often won or lost in that little extra bit that carries us home over the finish line.

In fact, I believe enthusiasm can make such a massive and positive difference to people's lives that it should be taught as part of a school's curriculum. After all, it's one of the key attributes that smart employers look for. (It's certainly something I place huge value on when I'm choosing expedition members.)

Imagine interviewing a candidate who says they love getting up early and being the first into work, and they love warming up people's days with a smile and getting their colleagues a cup of tea to cheer them up. That all they want is the chance to show you how hard they can work and how they will always go the extra mile.

Wow! You'd be like, right, when are you free? I'd give that person a shot over the candidate with the better A-level results any day.

So how do you teach it?

Well, you reward it and lead by example, for a start.

Encouraging enthusiasm is one of the most important things I do in my work with the Scouts. If I can get the message across to kids who might not be doing all that well at school that they can distinguish themselves and get A+ in the game of life by being enthusiastic in all they do – especially when times are tough and others are moaning – I know I can make a critical difference to their future.

Success almost always follows great attitude. The two attract each other.

You may not be the fastest, the fittest, the cleverest or the strongest, but there's nothing to stop you from being the most enthusiastic person you know. Nothing at all, except your willingness to step up and be a little different from the crowd.

So make enthusiasm a daily decision, even when you don't feel like it. We can all choose our attitude, and one of the best reasons for choosing positive attributes is the alternative – which means if you don't pick a good attitude, then you've got a bad one, or, even worse, a lukewarm, insipid, neutral one.

If you have to have any type of attitude to tackle each day, you might as well choose to make it a great one and make enthusiasm a driving force for good in your life.

People will love you for it, and remember you for it.

After all, who doesn't like to work with enthusiastic people?

I know I do.

6.
SAY
YES

A big part of getting ahead in life is a willingness to say 'Why not?' when others just say 'Why?'

In my experience, many people cross their arms, sit back and say 'Why should I?', and then let great possibilities slip by them.

A champion in life always goes against the grain and takes the path less trodden. And that means learning to say 'Why not?' instead of 'Why?'

This is especially important in the early days of building a career or following a dream. You have got to get out there and get busy opening up lots of oysters in search of that pearl. **You have got to try different things, meet loads of people, take people up on crazy offers and generally get busy living!**

It's almost always better, especially in the early stages, to say yes and to try something, rather than saying no because you fear where a yes will take you.

More often than not, saying no means that nothing will change in your life. A yes, however, has the power to create change. **And change is where we create room for success.**

And, by the way, the only person who likes change is a baby with a wet nappy! Change is scary and often uncomfortable, but life begins outside our comfort zone, so learn to embrace it and get used to it. Champions have to do that every single day.

A few years ago, I led an expedition to return to Mount Everest, the mountain I had climbed aged 23, a mountain where I had risked everything and survived – just. I had always held a secret dream to return and attempt to fly over the mountain in a small one-man paramotor – like a paraglider, only with a backpack engine strapped to your body.

At the time, the highest altitude that one had been flown was around 17,000 feet (5,180 metres). But being an enthusiast (and an optimist!), I reckoned we shouldn't just aim to break the record by a few feet, I thought we should go as high as it was possible to go, and in my mind that meant flying over the height of Mount Everest. This in turn meant we needed to build a machine capable of flying to over 29,000 feet (8,840 metres).

Most of the people we spoke to about this thought a) we were crazy, and b) it was technically impossible. What those naysayers hadn't factored in was the power of yes, and specifically the ability to build a team capable of such a mission. This meant harnessing the brilliance of my good friend Gilo Cardozo, a paramotor engineer, a born enthusiast, and a man who loves to break the rules – and to say yes.

Gilo was – and is – an absolute genius aviation engineer who spends all his time in his factory, designing and testing crazy bits of machinery.

When people told us that our oxygen would freeze up in minus 70°, or that at extreme altitudes we would need such a heavy engine to power the machine that it would be impossible to take off, or that even if we managed to do it, we would break our legs landing at such speed, Gilo's response was: 'Oh, it'll be great. Leave it with me.'

No matter what the obstacle, no matter what the 'problem', Gilo always said, 'We can do this.' And after months in his workshop, he did eventually build the machine that took us above the height of Everest. He beat the naysayers, he built the impossible and by the Grace of God we pulled it off – oh, and in the process we raised over $2.5 million for children's charities around the world.

You see, dreams can come true if you stick to them and think big.

So say yes – you never know where it will lead. And there are few limits to how high you just might soar.

7.
TO BE BRAVE, YOU FIRST MUST BE AFRAID

Being brave isn't about not feeling scared. Real courage is all about overcoming your fears.

There is little courage involved in setting out on a journey where the destination is certain and every step in between has been mapped in detail. Bravery is about leaving camp in the dark, when we do not know the route ahead and cannot be certain we will ever return.

While I was serving in the military, I suffered a free-fall parachuting accident in Southern Africa, where I broke my back in three places. I then spent 18 months back in the UK, in and out of military rehabilitation, desperately trying to recover. It was the hardest, darkest, most frightening time I had ever known.

Nothing was certain, every movement was agony and my future hung in the balance. No one could tell me whether I would even walk properly again. It had been a jump that had cost me my career, my movement and almost my life. The idea of ever jumping again was almost impossible for me to face.

Yet over seven seasons of *Born Survivor* and *Man Vs Wild*, I have since had to jump out of almost every aircraft imaginable: hot-air balloons, military C-130 cargo planes, helicopters, bi-planes, old World War Two Dakotas. You name it: the list is long. And each time it is still hard for me.

I never sleep much the night before, and I have recurring nightmares from my accident, which predictably surface just before a jump. It is a real mountain in my mind, one that induces a deep gnawing fear. Heart racing, sweaty palms, dry throat. But I have to force myself to feel that fear and do it anyway. It is my work.

The crew on the adventure TV shows I have done know that skydiving is hard for me. And I know there will always be a hand that reaches across to my shoulder during the few moments before that plane door opens. The team know I am busy facing demons every time we go up, but it is the job, and I don't ever want to let my demons win.

Bravery is about facing up to the things we fear the most, and overcoming and conquering those fears…or at least quelling them for a while.

And the greater the fear, the greater the bravery.

But one thing I know for sure: it is only by doing what we fear that we can ever truly learn to be brave.

8.

'THEM THAT STICK IT OUT ARE THEM THAT WIN'

Behind every successful person you'll undoubtedly find a string of failed attempts. We might not always notice the failures (as the successes tend to blind us to them), but to get to the success, those people will inevitably have had to walk through a good number of 'failures' first.

It is just the way of the world: to get to the successes, you have got to get out there and commit to fail a few times first.

The key is not in the failures themselves, but in your ability to keep going. As Winston Churchill said: 'Success is the ability to go from one failure to another with no loss of enthusiasm.'

And it's been my experience that the real difference between successful and unsuccessful people is simply the dogged ability to keep going.

Like enthusiasm, the determination to see things through to the very end is frequently a more important factor in being successful than any qualifications or letters after your name.

I know from my own life that things would have been radically different if I hadn't committed to push through the many lows and failures along the road, and I now treat those lows as markers that I am doing something right!

For instance, I had – quite literally – hundreds and hundreds of letters of rejection when I tried to get sponsorship for my attempt on Everest. It was so discouraging to wake up to every day: another no, another blank. And many times I was tempted to give up the dream.

But I was also determined that I was going to climb that mountain. So I didn't stop. I kept knocking on those doors and writing those letters – and guess what? Eventually I raised the funds I needed to undertake the expedition.

Likewise, most people don't realize that I failed SAS selection the first time round.

People don't talk about the failure – they only tend to remember the success.

SAS selection is tough to do once, but it is even harder the second time – knowing how physically and mentally exhausting the process you have to go through will be. Not many are willing to go through it twice, because it hurts.

But I had made a conscious decision to give this thing everything.
I was totally committed to the outcome, whatever the pain.

So I lined up – again – next to another 140 recruits – again – in the full knowledge that only a handful of us would be there by the end. I was willing to give it my all for as long as it took.

Eleven months later, and a whole host of sweat, pain and sleep deprivation later, I was one of only four to pass and join the regiment.

You have got to be dogged and fail a few times in life to get to where you want to go. Get used to failure, and see it for what it is –

a
stepping
stone
to
success.

I wasn't fitter or stronger or smarter than those who failed – I was simply more determined to give it my all. I remember during selection, one recruit who had just quit turned to me and said, 'You know the difference between me and you, Bear? You're just dumber than me.'

He confused the ability to suck up whatever pain the selection process could throw at us with being dumb, when really it was doing what was necessary to pass – quietly endure the lows, in order to reach the highs.

Ultimately I made it through and that other recruit didn't – even though he was a much more qualified and experienced soldier than I was at that stage.

You see, if you quit, you lose. But so long as you stick it out, you're still in with a chance.

Life rewards the dogged, not the qualified.

As Harrison Ford once said: 'Them that stick it out are them that win.'

9.
THAT
LITTLE
BIT
EXTRA

Have a guess what the difference is between a £1 million racehorse and a £100 racehorse.

Well, obviously the £1,000,000 one is 10,000 times faster than the £100 one. Right? That's clearly ridiculous. Is it even ten times faster? No way. Twice as fast? Unlikely. At best, the difference is only ever going to be a few seconds. There is often just a nose between first and fourth place in a horse race.

And it is the same in life.

Champions and 'might-have-beens' aren't all that different: we all have one brain, one set of heaving lungs, a couple of eyes, ears and a mouth. Yet it is the little things that set champions apart.

A lot of horses, and most people, have what it takes to get them to fourth place in life. But the winners are those who know that when things get really hard and others start to fall away, that is the time to dig deep and give that little bit extra.

I will never forget the day I finally passed SAS selection. At the end of the long, gruelling process of elimination, where 140 recruits had steadily been whittled down to only four of us, I finally found myself preparing to get 'badged'.

Yet it was the most low-key event you could ever imagine. No fanfare, no bugler, no parade. Just the four of us that remained, standing in a small, nondescript outbuilding on the edge of the Hereford training camp; we were battered, exhausted, bruised and spent, yet our hearts were bursting with pride.

The commanding officer of the regiment walked in, stood in front of us and said these words – I have never forgotten them:

'From this day on, you are part of a family. I know what you have had to give to earn the right to be here. The difference between the four of you and the rest of those who have failed is very simple: it is the ability to give that little bit extra when it hurts. You see, the difference between ordinary and extraordinary is often just that little word extra.'

He then added: 'The work I am going to ask you to do now will continue to be arduous, even more so, in fact, but what makes our work here special is your ability to give that little bit extra when most simply give up.

'You gave more when others gave up. That's the difference.'

That short speech made a huge impact on me, and I never forgot it. The words were simple, yet for a young soldier, and one without a huge amount of confidence, they gave me something to hold on to.

And I have done that ever since, through so many hard times in jungles, deserts, mountains and life. That little bit extra.

Reaching our summits only requires us to hold on that little bit longer than most people are prepared to endure. Just that little bit extra, just that nose-length more.

10.
NEVER
GIVE
UP

If there's one person who understood the value and importance of sticking with things, it was Sir Winston Churchill.

Legend has it that when he once gave a speech at Harrow School, he simply stood up and said, 'Never give in, never, never, never. Never give in.'

He knew those simple words make such a difference.

Whatever your walk in life, the ability to dig in and not quit when it gets tough will not only set you apart, it will set you up for a more exciting, more fulfilled and more prosperous life.

That dogged resolve, that never-say-die attitude, takes people to a place that few are prepared to explore. And it is here that life becomes most interesting.

So, when you think you've exhausted all possibilities, look inwards and just remember one thing: you haven't!

You always retain the ultimate decision whether or not to hang on in there. No one can force you to quit. And luckily Churchill knew that this tenacity had power.

'Never give in, never, never, never. Never give in.'

He didn't need to say any more during that speech.

They were the wisest few words he could ever have imparted to those pupils – and it was a lesson learnt the hard way, at the bleak coalface of war.

Never give in, never, never, never. Never give in.

11.
THERE IS NO EDUCATION LIKE ADVERSITY

In 1941, as Britain was in the darkest days of World War Two, Churchill told a generation of young people that 'these are great days – the greatest days our country has ever lived'.

But why was Churchill telling them that those bleak, uncertain, life-threatening and freedom-challenging days were also the best days of their lives?

He knew that it's when times are tough, when the conditions are at their worst, that we learn what we are truly capable of.

There are few greater feelings than finding out you can achieve more, and endure more, than you had previously imagined, and it's only when we are tested that we realize just how brightly we can shine.

It's a cliché, but it's true: **diamonds are formed under pressure. And without the pressure, they simply remain lumps of coal.**

The greatest trick in life is to learn to see adversity as your friend, your teacher and your guide.

Storms come to make us stronger.

No one ever achieves their dream without first stumbling over a few obstacles along the way. Experience teaches you to understand that those obstacles are actually a really good indication that you are on the right road.

Trust me: if you find a road without any obstacles, I can promise you it doesn't lead anywhere worthwhile.

So, embrace the adversity, embrace the obstacles, and get ready for success.

Today is the start of the greatest days of your life...

12.
KNOW YOURSELF

The most sacred place in the ancient world was the oracle at Delphi in central Greece. Kings, warriors and envoys travelled from across the known world to hear the prophecies of the oracle.

Above the gates at Delphi, a short inscription greeted every weary traveller:

Know thyself.

This simple advice was considered the most important piece of knowledge anyone could possess. And to understand what the oracle told you, you first had to understand yourself.

There is good reason for this: if we do not know our own mind, our dreams, strengths and failings, how can we reach the heights we seek? We become like a ship with no rudder.

Which is why knowing yourself is so important: it helps you make decisions that make you happier, because you end up pursuing goals that are true to your very nature and core.

So how do you get to know yourself?

The first way is to spend some time alone – just you – without all the outside influences of peers and family that so powerfully shape our aspirations. Give yourself enough time to hear your own heart's desires, rather than being drowned out by what others want you to do with your life.

I am sure the advice your family gives you is motivated by great love, but that doesn't necessarily mean their advice about your aspirations and career is right for you.

This is your life. Be bold with it. Live it with energy and purpose in the direction that excites you. Listen to your heart, look for your dreams: they are God-inspired.

You will find that you have certain core competencies, things you naturally find you are good at. Look to those skills, feed them. Your purpose, dreams and aspirations will often be aligned with your natural core competencies.

Listen to what the Bible says:

You are wonderfully and powerfully made.

In other words: it is no accident you are good at certain things!

The second way to get to know yourself is to test yourself. Throw yourself into new challenges. Set yourself hard tasks. Find out what makes you come alive and test what you're capable of.

Before I climbed Everest, I saved up to make an attempt on a peak called Ama Dablam, one of the classic and more technically difficult climbs in the higher Himalayas. For many of the weeks I was there, I climbed alone, plugged into my headphones and utterly absorbed in each step, each grip.

I was in tune with myself. I was in tune with the mountain. It was just the mountain and me.

During those times, I really had the chance to push my own boundaries a little. I found myself probing, being willing to push the risk envelope a bit.

I started to reach a little further for each hold, finely balanced on my crampons, taking a few extra risks – and I made swift, efficient progress. I was exploring my climbing limits and loving it.

When I reached the summit and watched in awe as the distant peak of Everest came into view, ten miles to the north, I knew I had the skills to scale that mountain, too.

William Blake said:

Great things are done when men and mountains meet. This is not done by jostling in the street.

He was right. We need time and space and adversity to really get to know ourselves. And you don't always find that in the grind, when your head is down and you are living someone else's dreams.

Wherever you are in your life, it is possible to find your own challenge and space. You don't have to go to the jungle or the Himalayas – it is much more a state of mind than a physical location.

Mountains of the mind are around us all everywhere. And it is when we test ourselves that we begin to know ourselves.

13.
YOU CAN'T BECOME A HORSEMAN UNTIL YOU'VE FALLEN OFF A HORSE

When I was a kid, my dad and I would often rent a couple of horses and go riding on the beaches of the Isle of Wight where I grew up. They are some of my best childhood memories, even though there were many times I fell off on to the hard wet sand.

But just as I was about to burst into tears, my dad would then start to applaud me.

Applaud the fall?

But why?

Dad wanted me to understand that I could only become a horseman if I had fallen off a horse a few times – that we only become good at something when we do it enough.

That means there will be times when we get thrown off and find ourselves face down in the mud.

Life is much the same.

It's a vital lesson for almost any path we choose to take in life: whatever you want to do, the chances are that if it is worth doing it will be difficult. We all fall off a few horses. And getting thrown to the ground by the unexpected is a big part of learning how to ride.

It is how to get good at something – don't be afraid to make mistakes.

So see the inevitable setbacks and mishaps as vital parts of the learning process.

The stumbles teach us more about how to stay up than they do about falling down.

14.
PACK LIGHT

This brings us to the stage of our journey where I can begin to equip you with some of the key 'know-how' to help you survive the many obstacles that lie ahead.

Now, there is 'good' kit we need to carry and then there is 'bad' kit. The 'good' is the list we are going to start compiling. The 'bad' is the stuff we are going to drop. Ultimately I want you to be empowered with a super-efficient, totally functional kit list made up of solid principles on which to build your life and adventure.

And here is the reason why we want to keep our kit list light:

On an expedition, obviously you never want to carry more gear than you need. Unnecessary kit is just extra weight – and too much baggage slows you down. Part of the appeal of the TV shows I do is that they show how you can survive with just a bottle of water, a decent knife and some key know-how.

The message is that attitude is king and the greatest resource we have is inside of us all. Pack the right skills, and the right attitudes, and you don't need much else.

You can usually tell who the novices are on an expedition because they are the ones with the biggest packs, full of too much cooking gear, clothing and superfluous supplies they just won't use. Every day, they lug around the extra weight, and when it's wet and they're cold and they're at the end of their rope, that extra burden can prove the final straw.

I have seen it all too often: on Scout trips, big expeditions and on TV shoots.

The art of packing efficiently is an essential part of a successful expedition. And it's true in life, too.

But first up we need to look at how most of us 'gear up' for life.

So many people I have met over the years walk around carrying a heap of emotional hang-ups that weigh them down.

Maybe it's the burden of parental expectations that makes them pick a job based on what they felt they 'should' do rather than would 'love' to do. Or maybe it is a deep-rooted fear about the future, or an anxiety about what people might think of them if they choose a more unusual or less 'celebrated' or money-generating profession.

Whatever the 'baggage' is, those people lug this unnecessary burden around, determined subconsciously to live out their lives in such a way as to endorse what some key influencers have told them about themselves over the years. Even if those 'home truths' aren't true!

So many people have been told too many negative things from a very young age, and these shape us.

'You're no good, you're stupid, you're a failure, a disgrace...' the list goes on. But they are not true.

I am here to say that this burden doesn't have to forge your reality.

Yes, maybe you failed at something. So what? Who hasn't? That doesn't make you a failure. 'You're stupid.' No, you are not. You just failed an exam because you probably didn't work hard enough!

So, can you see some common solutions?

For the failures – keep trying. For the exams – work harder. Both are qualities you can influence. That's the good news. And as for the names you were called – believe me, they aren't you, and you don't have to wear those labels any longer.

Start afresh. Drop them. Pack light.

15.
SHEDDING THE HEAVY UNNECESSARY

So, before we go too much further, now is a good chance to acknowledge that maybe, just maybe, we are all a little guilty of sometimes living someone else's aspirations for us instead of our own.

And this is a great time to say 'No more!' to living out of fear and other people's expectations.

It is never an easy time to face some of those old negative feelings, but it is always a good time to change the way we pack and what we choose to carry further down the road of our lives and adventures.

Ultimately, the more 'bad' equipment we carry, the slower we go and the less far we travel.

Each of us gets to choose.

But when we shed the bad and travel lighter, a few things happen.

First up, I bet that you will laugh more, you will worry less and you are much more likely to achieve your dream.

Travelling light also keeps us free to adapt our adventures or careers. Free to listen to the calling. How often do great opportunities come to people, but they are too 'busy' or maybe too cynical to even notice them, let alone walk through an exciting new doorway.

Winston Churchill (him again!) once said words to the effect that everyone gets the chance to make their fortune once, but not everybody takes it.

If you're weighed down, head down and bunged up with emotional junk, you might miss that chance.

So look wisely at the 'baggage' you carry and your attitudes to the world. They will define you.

Do they enhance your life and increase your chances of reaching your dream, or do they hold you back?

A good packer is a tough packer. So be shrewd and be robust: if it isn't going to help you, leave it behind, throw it out. Stay light.

We change our beliefs and attitudes inch by inch in the small, everyday things. When you find yourself thinking about someone or something in the same old negative way, just stop yourself.

Think.
Check.
Change.
Refresh.

Job done. Smile. Move on.

Do this enough times and you will change. For the better;
for the stronger.

The Scouts' motto is simple: Be prepared. So, if you really want to
be prepared for whatever life has to offer, pack light, stay nimble, pack
the positive, ditch the negative, and seize your chances when they
come along.

That is so often how we set ourselves up for great adventures.

16.
WORRY
WORRIES

One of my oldest buddies from Everest and the SAS, Mick Crosthwaite, once gave me this sound advice: 'Don't worry about anything that's outside your sphere of influence.'

Or in other words: **if you can't change it, don't fret it.**

Think about it. What do you worry most about? Is it inside or outside your sphere of influence? You see, most of us fret and panic about stuff we have no control over – things we can't change.

Mick's advice made me realize that if I can't change it, I just won't worry about it. Instead, spend the time and mental energy effecting positive change where you can, not where you can't.

It is sound advice, but it isn't how most people live.

Mark Twain famously said that he had spent most of his life worrying about things that never happened. I think people probably do this a lot. It is partly why so few get to where they dream of. They dare not… just in case.

Fears and worries – about things that are long passed, or that may never materialize in our future – all weigh us down and slow us up.

So where you can, drop the worries.

Jesus talked a lot about this, and this was a guy who had some serious reasons to worry. After all, he was about to be tortured to death on a cross, bearing the pain and burden of every bad deed and thought ever done by mankind. Now that is a proper-sized weight to carry!

But yet he still said: 'Cast your burdens on to me, for I care for you.'

That verse is a good thing to remember, and it has helped me so many times to overcome some pretty big worries.

Even if you find it hard to believe for yourself, and even if you haven't quite figured out all the theological details, just try it for the heck of it! What do you have to lose, apart from a little pride? (And pride is never a great thing to have too much of anyway.)

So just claim Christ's promise over your concerns. Close your eyes and pass them upstairs to Him. **He has developed an awesome habit over the last few thousand years of answering simple, honest, heart-led prayers.**

Pass them up, then let them go.

And one final word on worrying. Remember this: **The past is history, the future a mystery but the 'now' is a gift – that's why we call it the Present.**

You must learn to live in the Present.

Embrace it, relish it, work it, cherish it.

It doesn't last for ever.

17.
TENTS DON'T REPAIR THEMSELVES

On my first-ever mountaineering expedition – a school trip to Snowdonia – I learnt a very valuable lesson about tents, and about life, too.

We reached the campsite after midnight and it was raining hard. We were all tired and wet and were desperate to get our tents up and get inside. In our rush – and inexperience – we did it as quickly as possible, cut lots of corners, clambered inside, and, sure enough, at about 3 a.m. it all started to go wrong.

I was woken by the sound of the first peg snapping, followed by that soft, soggy sound of wet canvas collapsing. It's OK, I told myself – at least the other pegs are still in place.

So my friend Watty and I rolled over, buried our heads in our sleeping bags and pretended nothing was wrong.

But the loss of tension from the first break meant that the rest of the tent was taking too much strain. With a dramatic snap and crack, the remaining pegs gave way.

Watty and I found ourselves in the pitch black, smothered by wet, cold canvas and lying in a puddle of muddy water. Everything got soaked, we got chilled to the bone, and for the rest of the trip there wasn't a moment when we didn't wish that we had done the job properly at the start – or at least got out of our sleeping bags when the first peg broke and carried out a repair.

The metaphor is pretty straightforward: if something needs doing, do it well.

My mum used to say:

When a job is once begun, leave it not till it is done. Be it big or be it small, do it well or not at all.

Smart lady. It was good advice, and it means that so much of what you do will be productive, rather than lukewarm mediocrity – the nemesis of success.

Doing a job right first time also gives you the assurance that anything that has your mark on it is done to the right standard: you don't have to worry about any small tears turning into massive rips. This in turn builds confidence. And when you're confident, you make faster progress.

So do jobs once, and do them well.

18.
PADDLE YOUR OWN CANOE

I love these simple words for life. Paddle your own canoe – they say it all really.

But how many people do you know who, when there is something wrong in their life, expect someone else to come along and fix it for them? It is so common: an assumed 'right' that it is someone else's job to provide for and nanny them. It is someone else's job to fix up the mess.

It is never down to us.

Now, don't get me wrong. Many people need help – for real – and our calling if we are to be 'successful' has to include loving and helping those who are suffering, struggling or trapped in a cycle of poverty, ill-health or violence. At the heart of real success is always giving (I am going to give this a whole chapter later on).

The sort of 'needing help' I am talking about isn't really needing help, it is called asking someone else to do the hard work. You could call it laziness.

There is, all around us, an expectation that someone else – whether it is the boss, the teacher or the government – will step in to solve our health, wealth and community issues.

One of the most valuable lessons of survival training is self-reliance: when no one is coming to the rescue, it's down to you to sort things out. There is a simplicity, an honesty, a self-awareness and a power to that.

You can no longer blame anyone else for where you are. There are no more excuses. **There is just a silent awareness that this is where you are, and that is where you want to be.**

Between those two points there needs to be action. A whole lot of it. Good, positive, daily action. Action when it is raining; action when you really want to lie in a little longer; action when all about you is crumbling or failing; action when all is dark.

Action is the key. Action has the power.

So get out your paddle, take a deep breath, smile and get going. And watch the journey unfold.

You are now living the adventure for real, master of your own destiny. You are no longer waiting for someone else to help you out; you are not expecting to be handed something on a plate. **You are your own rescue.**

Now you understand the phrase: 'If it is to be, it is up to me.'

It feels good, eh? Doing it yourself. Paddling your very own canoe.

Now it is all about hanging on for the ride!

19.
DON'T
ASSUME

You know that old saying, that to ASSUME makes an ASS out of U and ME? Well, it's so true.

Too many times on expeditions I've either been caught out myself, or seen others get caught out, by 'assuming' that someone else was carrying the right gear, whether it be a rope, food or fuel, only to find out that everyone had 'assumed' the same thing!

One of the reasons I love the time I spend on expeditions and in the wilderness is because every little thing matters. One wrong step, one missed opportunity or one lapse of judgement can be a matter of life or death.

You quickly realize you cannot make assumptions lightly. If your life depends on carrying the right supplies, or knowing that your parachute has been packed correctly, then you learn you cannot take such things for granted.

It's good training for the rest of your life, too. If something is important, always check – never assume. **You might look a little foolish if you always ask the basic questions, but better a fool than an ass!**

It's usually ego that stops us from asking the 'silly' questions, but I know a lot of 'smart' people on expeditions who have tripped over their egos and fallen flat on their faces.

When it comes to navigating on an expedition, this ability to be clear and un-'assuming' is especially important.

All of us have, at times, when navigating from A to B, had a few moments of doubt. 'Are we here or here?' we ask. The stubborn press on, 'hoping', 'assuming' all will be clearer in a mile or two. It rarely works like that.

Too many times, if you don't act fast, a small error in judgement can become a big error with desperate consequences – and that applies to navigating through life as well as through mountains.

A good rule with navigating is that if there is doubt, then stop, reassess, ask others for help if you need to. Trust me, a stitch in time saves nine.

We would all prefer to be asked than for the leader to get us lost.

Besides, I have also learnt that people generally like to help and love to be asked for their advice. **So put your ego aside and let people help you.** Anyone who succeeds is really standing on many other people's shoulders – the shoulders of those who have helped them along the way.

Assume nothing, be humble, and don't be afraid to ask for that little bit of help when you need it.

20.
DREAMS REQUIRE SACRIFICE

The simple truth of life is that to get the things you really want, you will have to give up something else that you hold dear – whether it is your 'easy' life, your evening bar sessions, your comfort food or your time.

Success requires sacrifice. Get used to it.

I decided to try for 21 SAS Selection while all my friends were still students. I was sharing this old house with some great buddies, and we had a pretty cool student life, hanging out, bumming about, chasing girls – you know the story.

It was a fun time, but I quickly realized that if I really was determined to make it through SAS selection, then some things, in fact many things, would have to be sacrificed. The student parties, the lie-ins, the curries, the wine, the worry-free living and the home comforts…

None of these things was going to be compatible with attaining what I hoped for by joining the UK Special Forces. But then again, none of those things would ever mean as much to me as the pride of achieving something uniquely special.

Few people try, because few people dare. And most don't want to give up on the easy.

Think of your favourite sports star. Let me tell you, they spent every waking moment of their teenage years in the gym, pounding pavements or knocking a ball against a wall. You just don't get good at something unless you dedicate yourself to it.

It's not rocket science: the rewards go to the dogged.

But sacrifice hurts, which is why so many take the easy option. But what most people don't realize is that sacrifice also has power. Knowing that you have denied yourself something you wanted often means you put even more effort into achieving your goal. It's the Yin for the Yang.

I like to see sacrifice as a type of fuel that powers you towards your destination. The more you give up, then the more energy, time and focus you gain to commit to your goal.

It's never easy to make sacrifices, especially when you know they are going to hurt. **But I would encourage you to choose the option that will make you proud.**

There is a great line in the poem 'The Road Not Taken' by Robert Frost that says: 'I took the one less traveled by, And that has made all the difference.'

Do you want to make a difference? Do you want to be one of the few or the many?

If you want to achieve something special, then you have to choose a path that most won't dare to tread.

That can be scary; but exciting. And there will be a cost. Count it. Weigh it. Are you really prepared to pay the price? The sacrifice?

Remember this:

Pain is transitory; pride endures for ever.

21.
FAILURE ISN'T FAILURE

I try never to use the word 'failure'. Because failure doesn't really exist apart from in our mind. I call it something else: 'an unsatisfactory outcome'. Or even better: 'a stepping stone to success'.

People are often quick to label others a 'failure'. There are many people who find it all too easy to point out loud and clear when others fall short of their dreams.

But only little people belittle other people. Look at whom President Theodore Roosevelt so smartly gave the real credit to in life:

It is not the critic who counts: not the man who points out how the strong man stumbles or where the doer of deeds could have done better. The credit belongs to the man who is actually in the arena, whose face is marred by dust and sweat and blood, who strives valiantly, ... who, at the best, knows, in the end, the triumph of high achievement, and who, at the worst, if he fails, at least he fails while daring greatly, so that his place shall never be with those cold and timid souls who knew neither victory nor defeat.

Cowards criticize mainly because it makes them feel better about their own lack of courage to try anything daring themselves. So the best (though often the hardest) thing to do is to ignore their criticism. Or, even better, use it as fuel to your fire.

We all face criticism and we all have to live with our 'failures', and other people's opinions of those 'failures', but try not to take them personally. Consider them as signposts that you are doing something right.

It means you are where you should be: in the arena, in the battle, and another stepping stone closer to success.

Edmund Hillary, Neil Armstrong, you know the names. Men who embraced the ultimate in risk and failure. And if they hadn't faced the risk and failure, then both Everest and the moon would have very different stories to tell.

You see, if it was all easy then everyone would succeed. **It is precisely the risk and the chances of failure that give us the opportunity for success.** And if you can fail more than anyone else you know, I just bet that you will finally succeed! Fail, fail, fail again. Sound strange? Well, it is a key to succeeding.

Go out there, take calculated risks, work hard, be ready for the break, and be prepared to run when everyone else is slowing down.

Then success will come knocking. It is a law of the universe and a wonderful part of how the world works.

22.
COMMIT TO 'FAIL'

Failure teaches us so much about ourselves, and about life, that we should welcome it. This might sound odd, but it's only when you are prepared to embrace failure that you can truly set yourself up for success.

You see, nothing worthwhile is ever easy. Every time you try and do something new, or something difficult, or unusual, you are absolutely going to get doors closed in your face, friends mocking you and phones slammed down on you.

Rejection and disappointment is going to come at you from all angles.

One way or another, you need to find a way to cope with that failure. I do it by seeing failure as a stepping stone on the path to where I want to go. **Every time I fail, I take comfort in knowing I'm closer to my goal.**

I remember hearing the story of a father telling his kid that in order to succeed, he first had to go out and fail 22 times – only when he had done that would they discuss success again.

Now, I'm not sure why he said 22 times exactly, but the attitude is wonderfully counter-society. The father knew that if his son failed 22 times, then along the way he was inevitably bound, at some point, to succeed.

Fail your way to success. Embrace it. All of those 22 opportunities to succeed.

We live in a world where dream-stealers tell us to be scared to dare greatly, because of the chance of failure and the level of risk. But all great adventures have risk and a chance of failure. That's the whole point – otherwise it isn't an adventure!

So get out there and get busy 'failing'...

23.
HONOUR THE JOURNEY, NOT THE DESTINATION

As a team, when we came back from Everest, so often the first question someone would ask us was: 'Did you make it to the summit?'

I was lucky – unbelievably lucky – to have reached that elusive summit, which also allowed me to reply to that summit question with a 'yes'. My best buddy Mick found the question much harder, as a 'no' didn't tell even part of his incredible story.

He might not have made it to the very top of Everest, but he was as near as damn it. For three months we had climbed alongside each other, day and night. Mick had been involved in some real heroics up high when things had gone wrong, he had climbed with courage, dignity and strength, and he had reached within 300 feet (90 metres) of the summit.

Yet somehow that didn't count in the eyes of those who asked that ironically unimportant question: 'Did you reach the top?'

For both of us, the journey was never about the summit. It was a journey we lived through together; we held each other's lives in our hands every day, and it was an incredible journey of growth. The summit I only ever saw as a bonus.

When we got that question on our return, I often got more frustrated for Mick than he did. He was smart and never saw it as a failure. He'd tell you that he was actually lucky – for the simple reason that he survived where four others that season had died.

You see, Mick ran out of oxygen high up on the final face of Everest at some 28,000 feet (8,500 metres). Barely able to move, he crawled on all fours. Yet at that height, at the limit of exhaustion, he slipped and started to tumble down the sheer ice face.

He told me he was certain he would die.

By some miracle he landed on a small ledge and was finally rescued when two other climbers found him.

Four other climbers hadn't been so lucky. Two had died of the cold and two had fallen. Everest is unforgiving, especially when the weather turns.

By the time I was back with Mick, down at Camp Two a couple of days later, he was a changed man. Humbled, grateful for life, and I had never loved him so much.

So when everyone at home was asking him about the summit, or sympathizing with him for narrowly missing out, Mick knew better. He should have died up there. He knew he was plain lucky to be alive.

'Failure' had become his blessing, and life had become a great gift to him.

And those are great lessons that many never learn – because you can only learn them through a life-changing journey, regardless of the destination.

Consider the billionaire who flies into the South Pole for an hour to 'experience' it, compared to the man who has toiled, sweated and struggled across hundreds and hundreds of miles of ice, dragging a humble sledge.

You see, it is the journey that makes the man.

And life is all about our growth, not our trophies.

24.
BEWARE THE THREE Gs

A pastor friend called Jamie once said to me that as a man becomes more successful he must always watch out for the danger of the three Gs. I was intrigued.

He said that the higher we climb, the further there is to fall, and that these three Gs have shown themselves to be successful people's undoing time and time again.

I wanted to know what these Gs were. He smiled and said: 'They are Glory, Girls and Gold. Look at the wealthy man who loses his family through an affair, or who loses all sense of self through the empty pursuit of more money or greater status.'

As you grow in your success, it is worth keeping an eye on what these three Gs stand for to avoid them ever becoming stumbling blocks.

Now don't get me wrong – those three Gs are not all bad! I mean, I am married to an amazing girl, we have earned some money, and along the way have received a bit of glory in terms of the occasional award or accolade. But it is when you get too greedy, too needy, or too unfulfilled without more G – that's where the danger looms.

The pastor's warning was that status, adoration and/or financial success don't guarantee personal success; **those 3 Gs – girls, gold and glory – are fickle masters.**

But how many of us as young men aspired to all three of those Gs when we started out on life? We are human, aren't we? We hope, and are led to believe (you have to thank the newspapers and glossy mags for this), that girls, glory and gold will all make us feel brilliant.

And they will, maybe, for a fleeting moment or two...

But in the long term, I promise you, none of them helps to fill that aching hole inside. Open up any newspaper and you'll find the story of a life gone wrong in the sole pursuit of one of the Gs, or, in the case of some high-profile footballers, sometimes all three.

But we also learn. And a wise man learns from other people's mistakes. That was all the pastor was wisely pointing out. **Learn from others, never get complacent and know where the classic old dangers come from.**

25.
SEEK OUT THE FIVE Fs

My dad always told me that living a good life was about 'looking after your friends and family and having the courage to go for your dreams'. That was life in a nutshell for him.

Luckily those simple values meant much more to him than my school reports – which weren't always glowing!

I have always tried to follow his advice, but I also adapted his mantra to take it one stage further…

So here is what I tell young Scouts or young adventurers who ask me what the key is to living a fulfilled life. I keep it pretty simple. I call them the five Fs.

Family.
Friends.
Faith.
Fun.
Follow your dreams.

None of them requires a degree, and all of them are within our reach. Just make them your priority, write them on your bathroom mirror, let them seep into your subconscious over time, and soon they will be like a compass guiding you to make the right decisions for your life.

When faced with big decisions, just ask yourself: 'Will this choice or that one support or detract from the five Fs in my life?'

Family – sometimes like fudge: mostly sweet but with a few nuts! – but still they are our closest and dearest, and, like friendships, when we invest time and love in our families, we all get stronger.

Having good **Friends** to enjoy the adventures of life with, and to share the struggles we inevitably have to bear, is a wonderful blessing. Never underestimate how much good friends mean.

Faith matters. Jesus Christ has been the most incredible anchor and secret strength in my life – and it is so important to have a good guide through every jungle. (Go and do an Alpha Course to explore the notion of what faith is and isn't: www.alpha.org.)

Fun. Life should be an adventure. And you are allowed to have fun, you know! Make sure you get your daily dose of it. Yes, I mean daily!

And finally, **Follow your dreams.** Cherish them. They are God-given, dropped like pearls into the depths of your being. They provide powerful, life-changing purpose: beware the man with a dream who also has the courage to go out there and make it happen.

These five Fs will sustain and nurture you, and I have learnt that if you make them your priority, you have a great shot at living a wild, fun, exciting, rich, empowered and fulfilling life.

And, finally, remember that the ultimate success in the game of life can never come from money amassed, power or status attained, or from fame and recognition gained. All of those things are pretty hollow. Trust me.

Our real success is measured by how we touch and enrich people's lives – the difference we can make to those who would least expect it, to those the world looks over.

That is a far, far better measure of a human life, and a great goal to aspire to, as we follow the five Fs along the way.

26.
THE WIND AND THE SUN

OK. A story for you. And if I tell it right, it shouldn't need any explanation.

One day the wind and sun got into an argument. As you do. The argument was over who was stronger.

The wind was convinced he was much stronger, and blew and blew, until trees were felled, cars upturned, and the sea was a raging cauldron of waves.

The sun looked on. It was an impressive display, for sure, all that bluster. But still the sun said he was stronger.

So the wind challenged the sun to a competition.

'See that man down there?' said the wind, pointing to a man who was walking calmly along the street during his lunch hour. 'I challenge you to force him to take his coat off. The first to make him do this is the winner.'

The sun agreed to the challenge, and the wind took up the task while the sun watched on quietly.

The wind blew and blew, stronger and stronger. But the more the wind raged, the tighter the man held on to his coat. So the wind blew harder, but the man bent over even further against the wind, gripping on to his coat for dear life and through gritted teeth.

Finally, exhausted, the wind receded – unsuccessful.

It was the sun's turn.

The sun smiled, then began gently to shine. Nice and easy.

The man stood up from his tight huddle, and he looked around. He walked on for a little until he spotted a bench. Then the man removed his coat, folded it neatly beside him and sat down. All smiles.

You see, sometimes the best way to make progress, when we hit a dead end, is to change direction, change tack. Try a different approach. Put yourself in the other person's shoes. What would make them happy?

Often the angrier we get with someone, the more entrenched and angry they become back. **Try just being nice instead! Talk to them, listen to them, go the extra mile to do something thoughtful for them.**

Because, so often, being nice wins over just being angry.

27.
TO GET, YOU HAVE FIRST TO GIVE

A lot of advice in this book comes from my parents, and I am always grateful for having been raised by two wonderful and smart people. So here's another gem from my mum:

If you want to receive, you must first look around for something to give.

As a kid, this was usually a pretty simple equation – she would only buy me a new toy if I selected an old one to give to the charity shop. (Quite annoying, I seem to remember!) But as I got older I realized that giving to get is actually one of the universe's hidden rules.

You want someone to help you? Guess what: if you've helped them in the past, they are far more likely to come to your rescue. You want to get a bumper crop from your veg patch? Guess what, the more water, fertilizer and attention you give your seedlings, the more bountiful harvests they will produce.

But the inexplicable thing about my mum's rule is that it works in the wilderness, too. **There have been many times when I've been lost, exhausted, hungry, and I've felt my strength and my ability to keep going draining away.**

In these situations, it's human nature to shrink back and give up.

Yet my mother's wisdom has been proved to me time and time again – to 'get' good results, you have to 'give out' something good or positive first.

So when I am tired, I commit to working even harder. When I feel downcast, I decide to be upbeat. You see, no matter how low your optimism or strength feels, if you can 'force' yourself to put out the good vibes, the good attitudes, the hopeful thoughts (even if you don't feel them or believe them right at that moment), then you will be rewarded.

Try it some time when you are dog-tired. Get off that couch and start moving energetically. You will soon feel invigorated. Or when you are knee-deep in paperwork, slowing to a crawl, try just picking up the pace and focus, get ripping through it, giving it your all – and your body and mind will respond.

To get, first you have to give.

Even in extreme physical or survival situations, maybe you and your hiking buddy are so thirsty you can hardly walk straight. Go on – let them sip first. Give them the greater share.

When you do this sort of thing, you will also somehow get stronger. It is as though the mental boost always outweighs the physical drain. It is how we are made.

Often I've been so scared that I have lain awake all night, terrified about what I am going to have to do or face the next morning to get myself out of the wilderness. So I decide that when it is dawn, I will be excited, smiling and focused, regardless of how I feel – I will be ready to throw myself 100 per cent into the task ahead.

In return, the wild has a habit of rewarding total commitment.

And when it comes to life and mountains, it is really very simple: what we put in is what we get out. And in order to get, we first have to give.

28.
EXPERTS SHOULD BE ON TAP, NOT ON TOP

This is another piece of advice from Winston Churchill (he was a fountain of great one-liners):

Experts should be on tap, not on top.

I have made the mistake all too often in the past of taking experts' advice as gold, as the only 'right' option. It has often been against my instinct, and it has all too frequently landed me in trouble.

To let yourself be guided purely by experts is always a recipe for disaster.

So-called experts might know their field, but they don't always know the whole picture of what's right. Especially for you.

I know some very wealthy people who don't even live where they want to because their accountant told them they could pay less tax if they bought a home in Monaco. It is as if their accountant has more of a say over their lives than their kids or partners do – and that is always a 'false' economy.

Experts are experts because they specialize in one small part of a field. A leader's job is to see beyond that, to see the whole picture and then to make a considered decision. The expert advice should be there to serve you: to be 'on tap', when you need it, but not as your only option.

So when you need guidance, 'listen' to all the experts, assemble the knowledge in your head, sleep on it, trust your instinct (more of that later!), then make an informed, not hasty decision.

By the way, the only thing worse than making a bad decision? Making no decision! So many people fail to get ahead because they can't decide. They dither.

It is natural. We all get fearful of making a bad decision – but really that is back to being scared of failing, and we know how to deal with that now, don't we?

Failing is OK. A bad decision is better than no decision.

So learn to make decisions – informed, good decisions, based on good advice, but not dictated solely by the advisors. Trust your instincts, and commit to your decision.

And if it proves wrong, then learn from the error, have the humility to acknowledge it, then move on – wiser and smarter.

And remember, like so many things, the more you practise making decisions, the better you will become at making good decisions.

You'll never have a 100 per cent gold strike rate, but some people get pretty darned close, and if you study their habits I bet you will see some clear patterns in their decision-making.

So, listen to the experts, keep them on tap, but know your own mind, know your own heart – and let these lead you to the right choices to keep you on top.

29.
INSTINCT IS THE NOSE OF THE MIND – TRUST IT

Instinct is almost impossible to define but it can be so important when we come to a crossroads on our journey through life.

Sometimes things just don't 'feel' right – even if all the outward signs seem to be pointing us towards a certain course of action. When that happens, listen to that voice. It is God-given and it is our deep subconscious helping us.

You see, we all tend to act in accordance with our rational, conscious minds. **But we have a clever, far more knowing and intelligent part of us that the smart adventurer learns to use as a key part of his arsenal – it is called our intuition, and no amount of money can buy it.**

Talented climbers and adventurers know that to reach a summit or achieve a goal we have to use all the 'weapons' in our arsenal – not just the obvious ones, like strength, fitness and skill, which many people rely upon alone.

Sometimes that final push to the summit requires something beyond the normal. So don't fight against that inner voice if it is speaking loudly to you. It is there to guide and protect you.

Listening carefully to this voice is how we distinguish ourselves from the rest of the crowd who so often barge through life, too busy or too proud even to acknowledge their intuition's existence.

I remember once in the Arctic, when we were attempting to cross the frozen North Atlantic in a small, open rigid inflatable boat (RIB), that I heard that voice very clearly.

We had been caught out in a monster, sub-zero, gale-force 8 storm, 400 miles off the coast of Greenland – and we were struggling. We were reduced to a crawl as we battled up and down huge, freezing waves and crashing white water.

It felt like only a matter of time before we would be capsized to our deaths in the black and icy sea during this longest of nights.

Each time one of us handed over the control of the little boat to another crew member to do their shift at the wheel, we had an especially frightening few minutes as the new helmsman fought to become accustomed to the pitch and character of those freak waves.

If ever we were going to be capsized, it was during these change-over times.

We got lucky once. We were all thrown off our seats after the RIB had been tossed up and landed on the side of her tubes, only to topple back, by luck, the right way up. We then got lucky a second time in a similar incident. Instinct told me we wouldn't get so lucky a third time.

'No more mistakes. Helm this yourself,' I felt the voice saying to me.

As I prepared to hand over to Mick, my old buddy, something deep inside me kept repeating, 'Just keep helming for a bit longer – see this team through the storm yourself.'

But we had a rota and I also knew we should stick to it. That was the rule. Yet the voice persisted. Eventually I shouted over the wind and spray to Mick that I was going to keep helming. 'Trust me,' I told him.

Mick then helped me all through that night, pouring Red Bull down my throat as we got thrown left and right, fighting to cling on to the wheel and our seats.

By dawn, the seas were easing and by the next evening we could see the distant coast of Iceland ahead. Finally.

Afterwards, two of the crew said to me quietly that they had been so terrified to helm that they were praying someone else would do it. I had been exhausted, and logic had said to hand over, but instinct had told me I should keep steering.

Deep down I knew that I had been beginning to master how to control the small boat in the chaos of the waves and ice – and that voice told me we might not get a third lucky escape.

It was the right call – not an easy one, but a right one. Instinct doesn't always tell us to choose the easier path, but it will guide you towards the right one.

Your subconscious intuition wants you to survive and to thrive. It isn't clouded by ego or others' opinions – those fickle things live in the conscious mind. Your instinct has a clearer purpose: to help you.

Listen to it. Learn to recognize it. Acknowledge it when it speaks and have faith in it.

Instinct is the nose of the mind. So trust it.

30.
STORMS MAKE YOU STRONGER

A lot of the advice in this book is about how to cope when things don't go well.

You see, life is unpredictable, and as sure as eggs is eggs, it won't always swing your way. But when those storms come I have a clear and simple mantra:

The time to shine is when it is darkest.

In other words: **when it is all going wrong, step up to the plate, give it your all, heave hardest on that rope, and show that you are bigger than the obstacle.**

Nature has a way of rewarding that sort of attitude.

Sometimes life tests us a little. Things we had banked on coming in just don't work out. People let you down, one disaster follows another. You know the phrase: it never rains but it pours.

When those times come we have a choice: do we cower and get beaten or do we stand tall and face it?

I liken it to the school bully. When you stand up to them, they often stand down. They are testing you to see what you are made of. Man or mouse?

So use those tough times as an opportunity to show the world and yourself what you are made of. Regardless of how you feel, how you see yourself, **I have learnt one key lesson from mountains and the wild: that underneath it all, we humans are made strong.**

We all behave and act a little differently, depending on how we have been brought up and what has been thrown at us in our lives – but the underlying truth is that the real core of each of us is strong.

I have seen incredible heroics from unlikely people on mountains. But it took exceptional circumstances for that bravery to emerge.

You see, we are all a bit like grapes: when you squeeze us, you see what we are made of. And I believe that most people are far stronger than they ever imagine. It is refined within us from thousands of years of having to survive as a species.

It might be dusty and hidden away, but it is there somewhere inside you: **the heart of a survivor. Courage. Tenacity. Strength.**

So don't shy away from hard times, they are your chance to shine.

Write this on your bathroom mirror:

Struggle develops strength and storms make you stronger.

31.
HUMILITY IS EVERYTHING

This chapter is about remembering your manners when things start rolling your way – as they surely will now that you are learning so many of these life secrets!

It's very tempting, when we experience a little bit of success, to think that our good fortune is down to our skill, our brilliance or our good nature. That might be a part of it, of course, but the truth is that every successful person has had great help and support from others. And the really successful person also has the humility to acknowledge that.

When you claim too much credit for yourself, or you shout too loudly of your success, you give people a really good reason to talk against you. No one likes a boaster. **And real success has humility at its core.**

I've been super lucky to have met some of the most successful sports stars on the planet. And you know what's interesting about the most successful sportsmen and women? The more successful they are, so often the more humble they are.

Listen to how Roger Federer or Rafael Nadal talk about their success. Even as the number-one tennis players in the world, they continually acknowledge their family, their coach, their team, even their opponents, as incredible people. And it makes us like them even more!

I guess it's because big-heads don't get our admiration, even if they are incredibly successful.

Why is that? Maybe it is because we know, deep down, that none of us gets very far on our own, and if someone says they have done it all alone, we don't really believe them.

Take a look at one of the greatest inventors to have ever lived, Sir Isaac Newton. In a letter to his great rival Robert Hooke, he wrote that his work on the theory of gravity had only been possible because of the scholarship of those who had gone before him.

'If I have seen a little further,' he wrote, 'it is by standing on the shoulders of giants.'

I instantly admire him even more for saying that. You see, all great men and women stand on mighty shoulders. And that means you, too. Never forget that.

There's a verse in the Gospel of Matthew that – regardless of your religious beliefs – we would do well to remember when we find our feet getting a little too big for our boots:

He who exalts himself shall be humbled; and he who humbles himself shall be exalted.

So if you want to be truly great, then walk humbly and talk softly – it is a sign that your success is real and that you have learnt that we only succeed because of the love and support we have had from many.

And make sure you walk your talk, as words without actions are empty.

Use your success to support those around you. Or, even better still, help anyone who wants or needs it.

Anyone you possibly can.

Now you are really on the path to greatness!

Get it?

32.
LAUGH AT YOURSELF

Everyone always warms to people who can laugh at themselves. It's human nature – and the best jokes are always against ourselves. It shows character, humility and grace.

So don't take yourself too seriously: if you fall in the mud, just sit up tall and laugh.

Conversely, note how those who laugh at *others* are the people we instinctively pull away from.

People who laugh at others are really showing that they think they're better than the people they're making fun of. And if they laugh at them, then we naturally think that maybe next time they will be laughing at us – behind our backs. And no one likes that.

The ability to laugh at yourself also shows to others that you adhere to one of the great teachings of the Bible:

Be humble, and consider others better than yourself.

Great people make you feel great about yourself. They build others up, they pay compliments often and freely, and they don't pull others down to push themselves up.

So laugh at yourself, not others; build others up before yourself; and talk well, not nastily, about others in public.

I love this idea: **How you speak about others speaks loudest about yourself.** It is so true (which is why there's a whole chapter on it later in the book).

It is one of my life goals that, at my funeral, those who know me will be able to stand up and say they never heard me speak badly of anyone else.

(By the way, I have failed at this many times already, but it is still a good goal to have!)

Like you, I am still a work in progress, but I am trying, like you, to do better. Every day a little kinder, a little more generous, and taking myself a little less seriously.

Great men and women never take themselves seriously. It is part of what makes them great.

Look at the animals: the strongest grizzly bear still rolls around with her cubs, goofing. It is part of their strength and magnetic appeal.

33.
KEEP GOOD COMPANY

Ever heard the phrase that you can judge a man – and a woman – by the company he keeps? I've already talked about steering clear of the dream-stealers, but there are other people that most of us have in our lives who do us no favours whatsoever.

If you've got a friend who's always putting you down, or always telling you that your ideas are naff, or who takes the mick out of your taste in clothes, music or books, then I bet you go home after seeing that friend feeling less good about yourself.

We've all had friends who turn up, open their mouths and spew out a torrent of negative junk about their lives.

Now, if someone came round to your home and emptied an actual bag of trash all over your sitting room, you'd go crazy – and you'd be unlikely to invite them round again. Well, we should do the same to those who dump their junk on us mentally.

Just because you can't see their negative verbal junk, it doesn't mean it isn't cluttering your life, and polluting your dreams and attitudes. Don't hang out with people like that.

If, on the other hand, you have a friend who laughs along at your same old jokes, encourages you to try new things and makes you feel good about yourself, then that's the person to spend time with. That's the positive junk! The good stuff.

The less you see of your toxic friends and the more you see of your enthusiastic friends, the better you will feel about yourself, and the better you will become. **We are such social creatures that we all tend to become like the people we hang out with. It is human nature.**

So spend your days in the company of people who build you up and who see your mountain as achievable.

It is why I pick team members on big expeditions so carefully. I don't pick people just for their skills – the world is full of skilful people. I pick those who have that rare combination of good skills and even better attitudes.

Those who see the glass as half full; those who will see an obstacle as a challenge not a problem; those who help others, who encourage others and who will watch my back when it is turned.

Picking friends and expedition members who are better than you is a sure way to grow yourself. It elevates us, it inspires us, and together we all get stronger.

But most people do the opposite: they pick friends or team members who are just a little 'lower' down the pecking order than they are, because it makes them feel superior. But that is not the path of growth – it is the path of mediocrity.

The true champion, the true summiteer, hangs out with those who help and inspire them to be even better – through encouragement, through their actions and through their attitudes.

34.
FIND A GOOD GUIDE

When you pursue an exciting path through life, you are – inevitably – going to have moments of hardship, doubt, struggle and pain. It comes with the terrain of being a champion – in whatever field.

So accept that fact. But don't despair, because the good news is that help is nearer at hand than you might imagine.

You see, if I am going to enter a difficult jungle or uncharted mountain range, I always make sure I have a good guide. Life is the same. Go it alone, by all means, but you make the journey that much harder. Trust me.

To give yourself the best shot of reaching your destination and achieving all you are meant to in your life, you need a great guide, someone who can lead you, inspire you, comfort and strengthen you – especially when the going gets tough, as it invariably will.

For me, my simple faith has so often brought light to a dark path, joy to a cold mountain and strength to a failing body.

And who better to have as a guide than the person who made the path or the mountain in the first place!

Psalm 121 says:

I lift my eyes up to the mountain; where does my help come from? My help comes from the Lord, maker of Heaven, creator of the Earth.

Good person to have on side, I always figure.

Now, some of you will say, hey, I don't need this Christian stuff. And I hear you. But it is easy to be cynical when all is going your way. Remember that. **But to have faith...that is much harder and takes much more courage.**

Robin Knox-Johnston, the round-the-world sailor, said: **'There is no such thing as an atheist in the Southern Ocean.'** What that says to me is unless you know what it is like to be truly afraid and have no one around to help you, then don't preach to me your atheism.

And, wow, it takes a proud man to say he never needs any sort of help or encouragement.

I sure need it.

But don't worry. Believing quietly doesn't mean you have to be all religious. I am not. And guess what...nor was Jesus! In fact, if you read about him,[1] he was totally fun, ridiculously free, crazily wild, loved a party and always hung out with the non-religious folk.

The only people he ever got angry with were the ultra-religious types!

Instead, finding a faith should help you to be freer, more full of life, more filled with joy, peace and love than you would ever imagine. And those qualities, in abundance, will only make you stronger and more capable of living a wild and adventurous life.

And what is even cooler is that Jesus turns out to be so much more than just a guide or a pointer of the way. He is also a backbone, a companion and a friend. When I look at my own heroes, I realize there aren't many leaders who haven't at some time quietly bent their knee and looked upwards for strength, resolve and peace.

Great men and women know their own frailty and have the humility to accept help to empower them to greatness. Be among their number.

Pioneers always take bold steps to explore new territory – you never know what you might find.

By the way, it is also good to know that faith isn't one-sided. As Christ said: 'I have come to seek and save.'

[1] I really recommend the book *The Jesus I Never Knew* by Philip Yancey to help get a better picture of this guy who hit Earth promising life in abundance. I mean, what the heck is that all about?!

He is out looking for us, too.

So be brave and let Him do his side of the bargain. **I call it the quest to be found.**

You have nothing to lose and everything to gain.

35.
SEEK OUT MOTIVATION

Over the years, I've noticed that people can be quite snobby about books like this. So-called 'self-help' books. They can be just as mocking of the people who read them or go to motivational talks.

Their main criticism of the kind of books and talks that motivate and inspire people is that the impact is often fleeting – that the effects of the book or talk don't last.

My response is to say: of course it is fleeting, of course it is temporary. But so are the effects of washing your armpits – that's why you should wash them every day!

Likewise with motivation – we have to have it every day. We have to fill ourselves up to overflowing with the good stuff, because the daily grind wears us down and dirties us up.

The trick with motivation is to make it part of your daily routine, like brushing your teeth or taking a shower. Do it, absorb it – every day.

So, drown out the bad with the good. Blast away the negative with the positive. Refill the jug as much as you can. Don't run your tank on empty but fill up at every possible opportunity with fresh, clean, good motivational fuel that will keep you soaring down the race track to the best of your ability.

It's not rocket science to understand that the more good we put into our mind and bodies (such as eating good, healthy food), then the better results we get out in return.

One of the books that has had the most influence on me is a little manual called *Rhinoceros Success* by Scott Alexander. I know, it's a weird title, but give it a read. I read it first when I was 12 years old and I still read it once a year to this day.

It teaches you in life to be like a rhino – to have a single purpose, to charge at obstacles and goals with total commitment and to develop a thick skin to deal with the slings and arrows that try to slow you down.

Still to this day, Shara loves to buy me things for my birthday with a rhino on. Lampshades, slippers, cushions, door knobs…you name it. In fact, it's become a bit of a family joke to get me the most obscure rhino trinket they can find. But it means that at home wherever I look I am reminded of the simple (and fun!) truths of the book.

They are all daily reminders to me to be a rhino in life.

So find a way, whatever way works for you, of making motivation part of your daily life. **Write notes to yourself on your bathroom mirror, keep a book that inspires you next to the loo, and feed your mind with the good whenever you can.**

If you do this every day, it'll soon become a habit. A good habit. One that empowers you every day to climb high, aim big, and have fun along the way.

36.
WE ALL STRUGGLE WITH MOTIVATION SOMETIMES

Shock, horror…yes, even I feel unmotivated occasionally!

I am human.

So don't worry when you feel a little demotivated – it is normal. Just give yourself a short break, take a nap, go for a walk, make a cup of tea, then pick yourself up and make the conscious decision to get charging.

It is always best not to deny to yourself that you might occasionally suffer from a little bit of stinkin' thinkin' – so give it its moment, then boot it out!

So don't beat yourself up about having a bad day – I have had loads of them and will have many more in the future.

Take a deep breath, pat yourself on the back for being human after all, then get out there and get moving again.

Champions don't stay down for long.

Oh, and I have a good trick for doing stuff, like exercising, when I really am not in the mood…I tell myself that I can quit, but only after three minutes. I have to at least begin.

Invariably after three minutes of running, I find I am in the groove and want to keep going. The hard bit is always getting going, so I commit at least to start, with my 'three-minute get-out clause'...which, of course, then doesn't get used!

Whatever works for you...but keep feeding the motivation into your brain and soul every day.

Remember the previous chapter on armpits!

37.
BE
KIND

Enthusiasm, ability and aptitude all have to be on someone's CV before I'll take them into a life or death situation, but when I am putting a team together for an expedition, there's one other quality I'm always looking out for – kindness.

Expeditions into jungles or across deserts or raging oceans are never easy. However much we might romanticize the lives of explorers, when you are in the middle of an inflatable boat with 50-foot waves all around, you haven't slept for three days, or you have been struggling with an injury in silence for a week, it is the little things that count.

What you really want from the people you are with is that they are kind – to know that they are on your side when the chips are down.

Let me give you a couple of examples: once you get above 25,000 feet (7,500 metres) on a mountain, and the temperature drops to minus 45°, if you don't get a headache – the kind that grips your head like a nut in a pair of pliers – then you're not human. Part of this is the altitude, part is the inevitable dehydration that comes from the thin air. So working hard 24/7 to keep hydrated is essential.

The only way to get water, though, is to melt the ice. But at that height, at that temperature, melting enough snow and ice to drink can take hours. **The good expedition member is the one who gives their buddies the first sip or the last swig of that precious water. In the extremes it is the little things that stand out.**

So try and look at all those sorts of moments as chances to distinguish yourself – and it is the kind, unselfish mountaineer who is loved and is often the real bedrock of a great team.

Another time, while on patrol with a small four-man team from my SAS squadron, out in the deserts of North Africa, we were waiting for a delayed helicopter pick-up. A 48-hour delay when you are almost out of water, in the roasting desert, can be life-threatening. We were all severely dehydrated and getting weaker fast.

Every hour we would sip another small capful from the one remaining water bottle we each carried. Rationed carefully, methodically. To make matters worse, I had diarrhoea, which was causing me to dehydrate even faster.

We finally got the call-up that our extraction would be at dawn the next day, some 20 miles away. We saddled up during the night and started to move across the desert, weighed down by kit and fatigue. I was soon struggling. Every footstep was a monumental effort of will as we shuffled across the mountains.

My sergeant, an incredible bear of a man called Chris Carter (who was tragically killed in Afghanistan; a hero to all who had served with him), could see this. He stopped the patrol, came to me, and insisted I drink the last remaining capful from his own bottle. No fuss, no show, he just made me drink it.

It was the kindness, not the actual water itself, that gave me the strength to keep going when I had nothing left inside me. **Kindness inspires us, it motivates us, and creates a strong, tight team: honest, supporting, empowering.**

No ego. No bravado or show. Simple goodness.

It is the very heart of a great man, and I have never forgotten that single act that night in the desert.

The thing about kindness is that it costs the giver very little but can mean the world to the receiver.

So don't underestimate the power you have to change lives and encourage others to be better. It doesn't take much but it requires us to value kindness as a quality to aspire to above almost everything else.

You want to be a great adventurer and expedition member in life and in the mountains? It is simple: be kind.

38.
NO ONE CARES HOW MUCH YOU KNOW UNTIL THEY KNOW HOW MUCH YOU CARE

My SAS patrol sergeant Chris Carter was the living embodiment of this advice, and if you are ever in a position of leading a team or managing people, following his selfless example will help you become a better leader and enable your team to achieve more.

Can you imagine how I felt after Chris had let me drink his last drops of water? Gratitude doesn't come close.

One of the regiment's toughest, most hardened of soldiers was showing that he was looking out for me way beyond the call of duty. And once I had been shown how much he cared, I knew that, in return, I would never let him, or the regiment, down.

That simple act of kindness, of caring, is always at the heart of great brotherhoods. Call it what you will: camaraderie, shared purpose. The end product was that here was a man I would work my guts out for. And that made us all stronger.

Ditto, on a mountain: the most important bit of kit or resource on any expedition is always the human asset. When valued and empowered, humans have proved they can truly overcome the impossible and scale the unconquerable. But first we have to be valued and empowered.

The real value of a team is never in the flash hi-tech equipment or branded sponsors. It's the people and the relationships between them.

As a leader, in whatever field, it is one thing for your team to see how much you know, but that knowledge isn't what will make your team great. What makes the critical difference is how you use that knowledge.

Do you use it to empower and support those around you? Do you value others above yourself?

Is your ego small enough, and your backbone strong enough, to raise others up high on your shoulders?

If you let people know, through your words and actions, that they really matter, that their work matters, that their wellbeing matters to you, then they will go to the ends of the Earth for you. Why? Because they know they can trust you to use all your knowledge, skills and power to support and encourage them.

You see, no one cares how much you know until they know how much you care.

39.
MONEY IS LIKE A RIVER: IT HAS TO FLOW

We live in a society where success is often (and falsely) determined by how much money we earn. Our culture values money way too highly, and here's why.

The *Rich List* that gets published each year sends out the message that having more money than the next person is something to aspire to. This has led to a culture where – once we have grabbed hold of whatever money we can – we hold on to it as tightly as possible… or else!

This same culture says that if you give it away then you will simply end up poorer. But the little-known secret of money is that it really works in reverse: it is only when a person starts to give away what he has that he begins to gain riches far beyond mere coins.

Let me tell you, accumulating and clinging tightly on to money will never make you happy. In fact, if that is your focus and your reaction to money, it will eat you up and make your life a neurotic misery. I have seen it too often.

Money is like a mirror: it reveals what sort of person we really are. That is where the real value of money lies – to distinguish the character of its owner.

Money is also like a river, and rivers need to flow or they die. When you dam up a stream, the water soon becomes stagnant. Likewise with money: stop moving it along or giving it away and helping others, and the money starts to go stagnant.

It first goes murky, then it dies.

Money has to be shared lightly, given generously, and used to enrich not just your life, but those of all around you. Only then does money have power.

Finally, money is like a butterfly: hold on to it too tightly and you kill it. Light hands, and a generous, free spirit, will make the butterfly soar, spreading joy and light wherever it lands.

It's not how much money you have that matters, it's what you do with it. That's how to become really rich.

Let me give you an example of someone who is ridiculously rich, in every sense of the word. Let me introduce you to Dave.

This is how Dave works: whenever he comes across great, everyday people, whoever they are – whether it's a shy 17-year-old just leaving school with a longing to visit his absent father who now lives in Canada; or a plumber who has worked beyond the call of duty, been respectful and diligent, but who rarely gets to see his kids as he works so hard; or a single mother, a friend of a friend, who is struggling to balance a million things and multiple jobs and wishes she could treat her kids to something nice – Dave steps in. A bit like Superman!

You see, Dave has worked hard in his life, and been rewarded with great wealth, but through it all he has learnt something far greater: that great wealth doesn't make you rich unless you do great things with it.

So Dave will secretly help people out in some special way. Maybe he pays for the young man's plane fare to Canada to see his dad, or for the plumber to take his family on holiday, or the single mum to get a car. Anything that is beyond the norm, out of the ordinary – he does it. And you know what? It blows people away!

Not only does Dave have the most loyal army of everyday people who would go to the ends of the Earth for him (and it is not because of the money he gave them, by the way, it is because he did something so far beyond the norm for them), but Dave is also the happiest man I have ever met.

Why?

Because it is impossible to live like this and not be ridiculously happy!

It is in the giving that a person becomes rich. And that can start today, whatever point we are along the road of our goals.

So don't waste a chance to get rich quick by getting busy giving.

Then stand back and watch the happiness unfold . . .

40.
FROM THOSE TO WHOM MUCH IS GIVEN, MUCH IS EXPECTED

When I left school, I worked for six months running a series of self-defence classes around London to earn some money so I could go backpacking. Finally, I saved enough to travel to India, where I had always wanted to go and see the mighty Himalayas with my own eyes. I knew it would take my breath away.

But it was the other things I witnessed in India that really blew my mind.

In the back streets of Calcutta I saw sights that just should not happen: legless, blind, ragged bodies, lying in filth-strewn gutters, holding out their blistered arms to beg for a few rupees. I felt overwhelmed, inadequate and powerless – all at once.

I sought out the mission run by Mother Teresa and saw there how simple things – cleanliness, calm, care and love – made a difference to those in need. These are not costly things to give, and the lesson

I learnt was simple: that we all have it within our power to offer something to change a life, even if our pockets are empty.

We've come to think of charity as being about big telethons or rock stars setting up foundations, but at its heart, charity is about small acts of kindness.

No matter the circumstances in which you were brought up, no matter what your job or how much you earn, we all have the capacity to give something – whether it's time, love or a listening ear to someone in need.

And the thing to remember is this: don't wait until you have more time, money or energy. Mother Teresa said: **'Never worry about numbers. Help one person at a time and always start with the person nearest you.'**

It is a great lesson, and the more we try to do this with whatever little we have, the more real success will gravitate towards us. People will love you back, your own sense of purpose and achievement will grow, and your life will have influence beyond the material.

That is a great way to be known and to live your life.

For the record: I am definitely still a work in progress on this one, but we all benefit from trying to aspire to this more.

So look around you for those in need – you won't have to look far – and your own life will grow in meaning.

Success is not success unless you live this one.

41.
NEVER
WORK
AGAIN!

There's only one place where success comes before work, and that's in the dictionary. Everywhere else in life, you do not get success without first working hard.

This is why it's important that you find the rewards you seek from the work itself. I would be climbing mountains and throwing myself off cliffs even if I wasn't being paid to do it – because **I love the sweat, the toil, the risk and the endeavour. It makes me feel alive.**

I can bet you that Mozart would have made music even if no one had listened. (In fact, he did, and for a large part of his life no one cared.)

If you love the process, then the length of the journey doesn't matter so much. So often it takes actors or climbers or musicians decades to find 'success', but they eventually triumph because they are working within their passion.

Do this for long enough and with enough enthusiasm, and 'success' will come. Even if it is not in the form you might first imagine.

A love of what you do is one of the highest forms of success you can ever have. If you do what you love, then you'll never have to do a day's work for the rest of your life.

42.
STOP
'TRYING'!

Maybe it's just me, but I don't like the word 'try'. *Trying* to do something just sounds like you're not really making that much effort – and the result is almost inevitable.

(I mean, what does it say about someone if you describe them as a 'trying' person? It means they try our patience to the limit!)

Somewhere in our brains the word 'try' gets associated with phrases like 'He tried his best' and 'Try again' or 'I'll try to make it'. It's almost as if *trying* to do something means you're setting yourself up to fall short of your goal.

So I swap the word 'try' for the better version: *endeavour*.

If you endeavour to do something, this indicates real intent, a willingness to stick with it, and an ability to see things through to the end.

Also, an endeavour sounds like you're on an epic, polar, life-or-death mission, which instantly makes whatever your task is more appealing!

Let me give you one of my favourite examples of the difference between trying and endeavouring.

When a new motorway was built, taking passing traffic away from Colonel Sanders' restaurant, his business crumbled. About to retire with just a paltry military pension, he was facing a bleak future. But the one thing he knew he had that was of value was a mighty fine chicken recipe.

He didn't have the money to open a new restaurant, but he figured he could franchise his chicken recipe to other restaurateurs and earn a slice of every chicken meal sold. After all, he had been selling his special chicken recipe for years in his own small restaurant: how hard could it be?

The answer was: very.

The first restaurant he went to politely asked him to leave with the words: 'We have a good chicken recipe of our own already; why would we want to pay you for another?' The same thing happened at the next place he endeavoured to persuade.

And the next.

But he persisted.

Guess how many no's he got before someone agreed to give his 'finger-licking' recipe a 'try'?

The elderly Colonel Sanders had to knock on 1,009 doors before someone gave him a yes and the legend and business empire that became Kentucky Fried Chicken was finally born.

Now, how many of us, after the first 50 no's, might have thought that maybe we should quit (or at least check our chicken recipe!)?

What about after ONE THOUSAND no's?

I reckon most people wouldn't even have got to the hundredth door, and long before they rang the 1,009th doorbell they would have given up. 'Well, we *tried* our best' would have been a fair assessment. But not for the good colonel!

Colonel Sanders – he really was an army veteran with some great military doggedness – had that spirit of determination, that *endeavour*, not to quit until he had found the thing he was looking for.

Trying often comes before failure. Endeavour more often leads to success.

But they are just words, I hear you say. Why does it matter whether we say 'try' or 'endeavour'?

It matters, believe me. **Our words become our attitudes and our attitudes become our life.**

43.
CHANGE YOUR VOCABULARY, CHANGE YOUR ATTITUDE

Our words have power. They have the power to change our lives for the better or for the worse. Even the Bible says:

The tongue has the power of life and death.

But what the heck does that mean?!

You see, I think 'trying' isn't the only word you should jettison from your dictionary.

Let's take the word 'problem'– that one instantly seems to me like a hassle and a pain. I replace it with 'challenge'. All of a sudden, something that seemed oppressive and negative becomes an obstacle course to be negotiated.

Changing the words you use will help you change your attitude to the situation you're in and the life you live.

Do you hear that? **The words we use become the life we live.**

That's why I have never ever had a 'cold' in my life. I have, though, occasionally had a warm! I refuse to call the weekend the weak-end – that symbolizes surrender. I call it a strong-end. (And I can guarantee you'll do much more with those 48 hours if you live it like that!)

And what about the words 'alarm clock'? 'Alarm' to me says emergency and that my life is in danger. That's a terrible way to start a day. I call it instead my 'opportunity' clock. Waking me up to give me the opportunity to get out there and grab life with both hands.

And then, of course, there is the worst of all…the word 'can't'. **When I hear an expedition member say it 'can't' be done, I can never resist amending it to: 'We haven't yet found a way to do it.'**

And therein lies the adventure!

When you start to use words and phrases like these, for sure loads of people will think you're crazy, but the good news is that you'll make them smile, and you will be talking into existence the sort of outcomes that most people can only ever dream of…

I'd take being called crazy to get that. Wouldn't you?

44.
LET THE MOUNTAIN GIVE YOU STRENGTH

This is something I couldn't quite get my head round when I was younger. One of my heroes, Sir Edmund Hillary, used to say that he drew strength from the mountain, and I just couldn't understand what he meant. Then one day I experienced it for myself.

Let me explain…

Mountains – and all the natural struggles and obstacles they present – are also arenas to find out what we are made of. **Inside every challenge, high on every mountain, is the opportunity to find a strength within us to survive and thrive.** It just takes us to be willing to dig deep and push on hard enough and long enough to find that strength.

But most people give up before they find it. This is why most people never reach the summit of their goals.

They quit when the winds pick up. They let their heads dip when it gets hard.

But I have learnt that on the mountains, the winds invariably pick up as you near the summit. (There is a scientific reason for this called the venturi effect, which means that as the wind hits the steep faces it gets squeezed, and when wind is compressed it speeds up. Hence windswept mountaintops.)

So don't be daunted or downhearted when it gets tough, don't shy away – step up to the plate, rise up to the challenge, and embrace the mountain. When we do this, the mountain will reward you, it will 'give' you the strength to overcome.

I don't always know where this strength comes from but I have often felt it within me. The tougher it becomes, the more I have felt this strength welling up inside.

So embrace that push, don't hide from the squeeze, but push on and allow the mountain to give you that strength.

Edmund Hillary found it, many explorers when really up against the ropes have found it, and I have found it. The key to its discovery is a willingness to push on and feed off the scale of the climb or the obstacle. Do this and the strength will come. Dig a little deeper, keep going a little longer, and somehow the summit will eventually come into view. It might not be until dawn, when the sun rises, but if you hang on in there long enough, it will inevitably come.

And so often the darkest hour is just before the dawn. You just have to hang on in there through those dark hours – don't give up, let the mountain sustain you and empower you, and you will experience the mountain within you.

45.
NO PLAN SURVIVES FIRST CONTACT WITH THE ENEMY

No matter how well you have prepared for something in advance – whether it's an expedition, an exam, a marriage or a race – when you find yourself in the thick of the action, however good your plan, things happen.

Adventure is unpredictable, and you had better learn to be flexible and to swing with the punches, or you will get beaten – it's as simple as that.

Mike Tyson famously once said: 'Everyone has a plan... until they get punched in the face!'

If the adventure is an exciting one, you can bet your bottom dollar you will get hit by the occasional punch in the face. **So prepare for the unexpected, and remember that forewarned is forearmed.**

Knowing that things will and do go wrong in the heat of battle is actually half the battle. It means that when it happens you are ready for it – you can react fast, stay nimble and you can survive the barrage.

We used to say in the military that when things took a turn for the worse you have to 'improvise, adapt and overcome'. IAO. It is a good one to remember. It gives us a road map to deal with the unexpected.

Being caught out, being caught off guard often makes people freeze – it is a human reaction to shock. But freezing can cost you the edge. So learn to anticipate the unexpected, and when it happens, smile to yourself and treat it as a solid marker that you are doing something right on your road to success.

If nothing ever goes wrong then you haven't been ambitious enough!

I also like to say that the real adventure begins in earnest when things go a little bit wrong. It is only then that you get to pit yourself against the worst the wild has to throw at you. When all is going to plan, with all the kit working perfectly and the weather benign, then it isn't really a test of character. It is easy to be the hero when all is going your way.

But when it all goes wrong and life feels like a battle, it is then that we can see what sort of people we have around us. It is only through the hardships that our character becomes forged. **Without struggle there can be no growth – physically or emotionally.**

So embrace the unexpected, feed off it, train yourself to be a master of the curve ball, and you will have built yourself another solid 'character' rung on the ladder to success.

46.
THREE
KEY
QUALITIES...

If I had to pick three key qualities to be known for and to carry in all personal and business dealings, qualities that will line you up for success, then these are them.

Live by these, and people and success will gravitate towards you.

Are you ready…?

1. BE A MAN, OR WOMAN, OF YOUR WORD

This is such a rare quality nowadays.

People make promises, vows and commitments so lightly, as if it means nothing to break your word, your honour and ultimately your power.

But if you can be known as someone who simply and without fuss does as he says, it will make you stand out like a bright light.
And people always gravitate towards the light.

It will mean that people will be able to trust you, they will believe you, and they will want to work with you.

Do I want beside me on a high mountain the man who will do as he says, quietly and with no fuss, despite the hardships, or the man who conveniently forgets, dramatically gives up or shirks from the heavy backpack or the unglamorous duties?

It isn't complicated, but it is hard to do sometimes. Especially when our feelings or circumstances conspire against us. But giving up and letting people down is always the easy option – the coward's choice.

Instead, make it a simple rule in your life: keep your word, honour your promises, and see your commitments through.

What a simple way to distinguish yourself from the crowd.

2. NEVER CHEAT

Most of us, every day of our lives, are presented with the chance to be honest or to cheat. Most of the time it is with tiny, inconsequential things, but it isn't about the 'things', it is about setting habits and patterns in our behaviour.

And if we are trustworthy with the little matters then it will be easier to be trustworthy with the important ones.

The one thing that makes me shy away from people is if I get a whiff that they are dishonest. Because if I see someone being dishonest with others, then I suspect they will be dishonest with me. And life is too short to have to deal with cheats, as they can all too easily rob you of your hard-earned success.

So have a good nose for people, and above all be honest in your dealings with those around you. People will notice it, appreciate it, and they will want to have you on their side.

3. BE GOOD IN A CRISIS

The final quality I list in the magic three is to be the sort of person who comes alive and thrives in a crisis.

Every adventure, business or mountain, will have a crisis moment – it is a prerequisite for success. There will be a key moment when the whole mission hangs in the balance...

This is your time to shine.

It rarely lasts longer than 24 hours, but how you react and act during those critical hours will often determine the outcome of the mission.

So be ready for it, think clearly, and act decisively.

Don't rest until the crisis is resolved. Be across everything, work non-stop and without relenting, until you see the ship through the storm. **Be the captain, lead from the front, get stuck in among the troops, call in all your favours, dig into all your reserves, and don't cease until you have steered the ship safely into port.**

This is your moment. Stand up tall, suppress your fears, grab the reins, and ride it home.

Oh, and however tempted you might be to panic – don't! That is always the worst thing to do, as it only serves to cloud your mind with fear. So if you sense the panic rising, kick it into touch. Tell yourself you need a check-up from the neck-up, and that you will not allow such stinkin' thinkin' – and then focus on the task in hand!

When you have come through, battered, exhausted but alive, take your wife or your team or your partner out, and go and celebrate! You deserve it. You have shown calm in the storm, resolve in the battle and fortitude in the crisis.

And once again people will remember that you are a great person to have on their side. Everyone likes to hang with the winners in life.

So there you go, those are my magic three qualities that are worth writing in your heart and mind. And as I look around at the champions I admire in life, in whatever field it might be, I almost invariably see those three qualities shining bright.

47.
BE A
VOLUNTEER

Something that is quite counter-culture, yet almost invariably betters and enhances a person's life, is to be a volunteer. It plays naturally into the life philosophy that 'to get, you have to give'.

When people volunteer their time and energy to help others, it invariably seems that in return they become richer, happier and more fulfilled.

As Chief Scout, I get to visit lots and lots of Scout groups all over the world. I get to meet young people full of hope and ambition and courage and laughter, who are out to make a difference. What an energy that gives off, and how inspired I always come away feeling.

There is something truly remarkable about the Scouts: this 28-million-strong worldwide force for good; the greatest youth movement on Earth, and all driven by great life-affirming values and a volunteering spirit. It makes for a killer combination!

At the core of it, my role as Chief Scout is to encourage; and I do that by getting stuck in, sharing as many skills as I can, and spending time just hanging out with young Scouts, encouraging their many hopes and aspirations. It is a voluntary role that involves giving time, love and energy.

But you know what? The truth is that I am the one who always leaves feeling most inspired. Every time. Amazed. Moved. Empowered and encouraged. This is what volunteering does for you. When you give, you receive.

Volunteering has always been a key part of Scouting, and to this day Scouts around the country promise to help others when they join up. And they do: almost half of all Scouts volunteer in their local community, from helping out in hospitals to protecting wildlife or visiting the elderly.

You see, you can't keep good people from doing good! It becomes like a spring, a well, overflowing. The more you give, the more you get.

I see volunteering as a character factory. It teaches us that there is more to life than having the latest clothes or getting a promotion. It reminds us that we're happiest when we work together for a common purpose that helps and empowers others.

Volunteering also takes you out of your normal environment and challenges you to do something new – maybe even something difficult. That is always going to help you grow as a person, as a character. **When we are challenged, we find out just how much we are really capable of, and our confidence increases with each new challenge faced and overcome.**

I know none of us has much spare time, but almost all the quiet, unsung, brilliant volunteers I have been lucky enough to meet are busy people. They are doers, they get things done and they just love to help people. They get so much out of their volunteering: so much that money can't buy and words can't quite explain.

But I have learnt that finding time isn't about the workload; it is often about the person behind the workload, and how they manage and order their lives.

So endeavour to be in control of your workload. Get the humdrum done first and efficiently to allow you to be productive and creative with the rest of your time. And make volunteering a small part of that time.

An hour a week can be enough to transform someone else's life – and then just watch how it will transform your own.

48.
ASK
A BUSY
PERSON!

They always say that if you want something done, then ask a busy person – and it is so true. Busy people are doers: they get things moving, they manage their time to fit it all in and they make things happen.

My buddy Mark is one of the busiest people I have ever met. He has four children, runs multiple Scout groups, volunteers his time for local causes, keeps fit, plays sport with his kids, takes his wife out on treats, has helped me manage endless expeditions and missions, and also happens to run the 24-hour crisis-response team for the railways!

Yet it all seems to happen in a very calm, managed, ordered fashion, with a smile and with purpose. What is Mark's secret?

He manages his time well and doesn't put off to tomorrow what he can do today. He tackles each day and every difficult task head on. He doesn't, like so many people, dodge the hard conversations or the painful workouts or the dirty jobs. **No, he picks the hard ones first, he gets involved, and he doesn't rest until that job is done.**

Mark hates half-done tasks. He says that they just clutter up his inbox or his to-do list. He prefers to start one and finish it, and only then will he move on to the next task.

I once asked him if he was always like this and he replied by saying: 'No way – but it all changed when I got invited to Fiji!'

I was intrigued. 'Why Fiji?'

You'll understand when you read what happened…

49.
GO TO FIJI ... EVERY DAY!

You see, Mark wasn't always the organized person he is today.

In fact, he says he used to start each day looking at what felt like the longest to-do list in history – he would sigh, then tentatively pick a few of the fun and easy tasks and slowly start to work his way through those before getting distracted by the doorbell, the kids, the boss or his stomach.

By the end of the day, the tough jobs remained undone, the list had grown longer and the fun had drained out of it all completely.

Know the feeling?

But then one day he got a phone call.

His best buddy called and told him to sit down and get ready for some great news. Mark was all ears.

Mark's buddy said he had hit the jackpot on a competition and had won two first-class tickets to Fiji, a week in a five-star hotel, all expenses paid, plus $10,000 spending money for him and a friend… Then he asked Mark if he would like to join him on the trip. Duh!

Mark was over the moon. He had always wanted to go to Fiji and was desperately in need of a holiday. He leapt at the chance.

The only small snag was that the plane tickets had to be redeemed in two days' time.

'Two days?' Mark replied. 'But I have the to-do list from hell and it would take me at least two weeks to clear my desk before I could go.'

But the date was set – meet it or don't go. The choice was clear.

That left Mark one day to clear his desk. He needed to do ten days' worth of work in one.

Early the next morning, before the sun came up, Mark was awake and downstairs, getting ready for his monster mission to get through his to-do list.

He made a quick cup of tea, did a couple of stretches, then hit his desk with huge energy and total focus. He had to get through this and get to Fiji, and he had to do it *today*.

That morning he worked like he had never worked before: he didn't dodge the hard tasks or just pick the fun ones. No, not that day. Mark started at the top and refused to move on to the next item until each task was done, completed, filed and closed.

He was like a rhino, attacking that list head-on with purpose. He had a holiday to go on. Any obstacle he came across on his list, he put his rhino horn down and charged through it, never taking no for an answer until he got the result he needed.

By lunchtime he was halfway through his monster work pile. He was so focused he forgot about lunch, and by 4 p.m. he had completed everything. Done. He leant back and let out a big sigh of satisfaction, amazed at how he had managed to do two weeks' worth of work in less than a day.

One thought crossed his mind as he sat there enjoying the fruits of his hard work, and it changed everything for Mark from that day on…

'Imagine if I had to go to Fiji every day!'

Imagine how much we could all do, how many goals we could charge down, people we could help, adventures we could have and promotions would be ours…if we could just set about them all with that Fiji attitude.

That's why I often say to myself when I have a lot on: It's time to go to Fiji!

50.
KEEP GROUNDED

When was the last time you ventured into the great outdoors? I mean really ventured, where you set out into the unknown with just a map and compass, backpack and sleeping bag – the sort of venturing that makes your heart beat faster.

Have you experienced the hypnotic patter of rain on your tent, the clear call of an owl or the rustling of the wind through the leaves at night? It's a feeling of absolute freedom and belonging – a chance to reconnect with both ourselves and planet Earth.

A night in the outdoors is also a reminder that the best things in life aren't things.

Money can't buy the quiet calm that comes from sitting beside a mountain stream as it 'tinkles' through the rock and heather.

Money can't buy the inspiration that you feel sat on a clifftop above the pounding of the ocean surf as it hits the rocks far below.

You can't bottle feelings like that.

And sitting around a campfire under a sky of stars is the most ancient and wonderful of human activities. It reminds us of our place in the world, and in history – and it's hard not to be humbled.

These sorts of simple activities cost so little yet they give us precious time to be 'still' – time to reconnect, to clear our heads of the dross, to remind ourselves of our dreams and to see things in the perspective they often require.

We all need that regularly in our lives – more than you might imagine.

My grandfather always had a little framed picture by his bed that simply said:

There is always music in the garden, but our hearts have to be still enough to hear it.

So every once in a while, take out your backpack and head off for a night under canvas. Even if it's only for one night, and even if it's only in your garden.

Nature and the outdoors are a universal and deep-rooted language that we can all pick up once we get immersed.

Once you have learnt to tie a bowline or cook a simple meal over a fire that you've built yourself, you'll never forget it. I mean, who doesn't want to learn how to make fire without matches? It is one of the greatest and oldest of human achievements.

These skills and experiences are so deep-rooted in our subconscious that it is no surprise that they calm us. It is about being true to who we all are. And to remind ourselves of this, every now and again, is always going to better our lives.

So camp out, enjoy some stories, watch a bit of nature's TV (that's a fire, by the way), eat simple food with your fingers, drink some wine and chat to those you love, and then lie back and soak in some quiet time under the night sky: it is restorative. You don't need to be in Fiji to get restored!

The only thing I would add to all this is once a year to watch a sunrise. It is good for the mind, body and spiritual health: to get up early and watch the sun appear quietly over the horizon, with no fuss, no fanfare – a gentle, warming, calm reminder that the world, at its heart, is wonderful, and that life is truly a gift.

Never underestimate the power of simple pleasures like this to restore and inspire you. It is part of how we are made.

51.
SCOUTING PRINCIPLES TO LIVE BY

The Scouts have some great life values as part of their heritage, which act as guidelines for young people to endeavour to live by. The values, or Scouting Principles, were written by Lord Baden-Powell when Scouting was founded over a hundred years ago, but they remain as relevant and empowering for us today as they were then.

Here are some that we should all take to heart.

First, the best-known:

BE PREPARED

My old sergeant used to say that if you fail to plan, you plan to fail. Time spent in preparation is never wasted.

Before we tackle any mountain, real or metaphorical, we have to arm ourselves as best we can – and that means preparing ourselves for what we face ahead.

Having the right kit and knowing how to use it when it matters makes a big difference. Can you put up your tent in the dark, against the clock? If you're a soldier, can you reassemble your rifle blindfolded?

A huge part of preparation is practice and, like they say, the harder you practise, the luckier you become.

If you practise enough you will get proficient; if you practise a lot you will become an expert. It is how we are made.

But then why aren't we all experts, you ask? Simple. Most people are too lazy to practise.

Remember that the will to win means nothing without the will to train. You have to get out there and be prepared to suffer a little if you want to be properly prepped for a big mountain or task.

Prepare physically, be fit enough, give yourself the best chance of success.

Prepare mentally, know what questions you will have to answer or subjects you will have to talk about, and then rehearse.

Practise, practise, practise.

And part of that preparation and practice should be visualization. It is one of the best weapons in any athlete's arsenal – the ability to rehearse in slow motion, performing the task perfectly in your mind. Visualizing like this opens up new neural pathways in the brain, so that when you face the challenge for real it is as if your brain has already done it many times before.

What a cool way to give yourself the winning advantage.

(Ask Johnny Wilkinson how important visualization was to him before he kicked the final winning drop goal in the Rugby World Cup final that time! He had already kicked that drop goal perfectly in his head thousands of times.)

What a great trick of the trade to have. Tiger Woods attributes 80 per cent of his golfing skills to visualization – and he hasn't done badly on the golf course.

So remember: preparation is key. Prepare well and wisely, and success will become inevitable rather than a matter of chance.

BE TRUSTWORTHY

This is one of the founding principles of the Scout movement, and one that is absolutely key to good friendships, good business relationships, and living a great life.

We have spoken about this principle before, when we said 'Don't cheat', but sometimes the big ones are worth repeating, so I don't apologize for throwing this one in again. I say it *and* the founder of Scouting said it – so it must be important!

Being trustworthy not only means keeping your promises, it also means keeping your word. **If you say you are going to do something, then you do it. Words are power, and people come to know us by the words we speak.**

A trustworthy person doesn't deal in lies and doesn't reveal secrets. Only speak the truth and never betray a confidence.

If you do this, people will learn to trust you. And when people trust you, they will want to have you around, they will want to work with you and you are guaranteed friends and adventures for life.

Get the picture? So be trustworthy. It is a great trait to be known for – and rarer than you might think.

BE LOYAL

This is another of the Scouting founding principles, and loyalty is something I prize.

Loyalty takes strength, because so many people get swayed by the crowd.

I remember a friend of mine, who also happens to be one of the most recognized faces in the world because of a TV show he hosted, who went through a career-changing moment when he made a very public mistake.

He was suspended from his job, his reputation was in tatters and the support from millions of fans and friends was all but gone. He had messed up big time, and he knew it.

But who hasn't? We all have. Many times. But for celebrities the pressure is intense. If most of us mess up, it tends to be a private matter that very few people will get to see. Because mistakes are embarrassing, aren't they? And trust me, I have made a few over the years.

But when the world gets to see your mistakes and cast judgement on them, it can be a whole different ball game.

I remember ringing him and saying, 'Keep your spirits up – who hasn't messed up? You've said you are sorry, and we are thinking of you and are here for you if you need anything, anything at all.'

The other end of the line went quiet. Then my friend very humbly said, 'Normally my phone doesn't stop ringing from dawn to dusk with "friends" and colleagues wanting stuff and sharing stuff with me. But, do you know, since I messed up, my phone had been like a corpse, no one has rung at all.' He paused. 'Thank you for caring and thank you for standing by me. It means a lot.'

Now being a friend and being loyal doesn't mean we have to condone mistakes. It's not about the mistake, it's about the human being. Being loyal means we act like a friend reaching out to someone in need.

I like the line that goes: **'A good friend walks in when the rest of the world walks out.'**

We live in a very fickle world where if we don't like something, then there is a great temptation just to bin it and replace it. We see this applied to so many things, from shoes to marriages. But the irony is that the more we seek perfection – in ourselves, in things, in others – the less satisfaction we find.

Loyalty seems quite old-fashioned, but the truth is that loyalty is more relevant than ever.

Anyone who has ever been let down by a friend, or, conversely, has ever had a friend stick up for them in a difficult moment, knows this to be true.

Ultimately, life is about relationships, and relationships thrive when we show loyalty.

And how we act in the big moments defines us, and how we behave when important things are on the line is how we are remembered and valued.

A Scout is the sort of person who shows loyalty, especially when it is tough. And people will always remember.

52.
LEARNING COURAGE

First up, courage has nothing to do with showy displays of bravado. Courage has everything to do with quiet feats of action over emotion.

Real courage is about how we react in the face of overwhelming odds. And it is impossible to be courageous if you aren't also afraid. Courage involves facing our fears, and walking through them.

It is *not* about having no fear, but it is about doing what is necessary *despite* the fear.

One of the bravest people I have ever met is an 11-year-old boy from Hungary, called Yosef. Yosef is battling a life-threatening disease and intense pain with a smile, determination and the warmest of hearts. Even though he is scared every day, and has undergone some 45 surgical operations in an effort to preserve his young life, he still chooses to tackle every day head-on with optimism.

That is real courage.

Being brave is rarely the easy option. If it was, everyone would win the VC. Battles – real and metaphorical – aren't like that. **Battles in life are scary. I know, I have been in enough.**

But battles also give us an opportunity to distinguish ourselves – they give us a chance to stand tall and show courage, despite the fear, trepidation and weakness we naturally feel.

Courage is the ace in the pack – the ticket that can break a stalemate and make the difference.

If we can, despite our feelings, take that courage pill and just get on and do what we hope we might be brave enough to do…then the world will often smile in return.

The world rewards bravery in the same way that the wild rewards commitment. Another law of the universe. **Be brave and the walls often crumble.**

Try it. Despite your feelings. And when you are in the midst of your battles, know that you have a choice. Be brave or hide.

(By the way, sometimes being brave means we have to hide. Discretion can be the better part of valour. There are many times when the brave option isn't the muscle-flexing, lots of smoke, and straight-up-the-middle option. Rather, it can often be the humble, quiet retreat – the admission-that-we-were-wrong option.)

Courage comes in many forms, but the common thread is that it is about finding the spirit inside us to do what is right, in the big moments, despite the fear.

The Latin root of the word courage means 'heart'. I love that. Showing heart when it really matters. Being courageous in those big moments in life that we all face.

One final thought: the most courageous people are also sometimes the most unlikely people. I have seen it many times on high mountains. Ordinary people, in extraordinary situations, having to be incredibly brave.

So take heart. If you don't think you're very brave – watch out! You're the perfect candidate.

53.
USE
TIME
WISELY

Unlike talent, or money, or luck, there is one resource that is distributed to every one of us equally. We each get 24 hours a day – and it is how we use those 24 hours that sets people apart.

Time is our precious resource. **Change the way you use your time, and you change your life.**

All our lives are products of the many daily small decisions we make. And how you spend a minute can dictate how you spend an hour, and eventually how you spend your hours determines whether you reach your goals.

So be wise with it.

People are careful how they spend their money, but are often less careful how they spend their time – **yet no man is rich enough to buy back his past.**

I find it helps me to make better decisions if I consider how I'll feel when I'm older. Will I wish I had spent more time building some corporation's dreams, or my own? And no one wishes at the end of their life that they had spent more time in the office!

Instead, people wish they had spent more time with their family, their children, their friends, and following great dreams. These thoughts guide my choices.

Likewise, if we are lazy, or waste too much time watching TV or playing video games, we know we are not going to have much to look back on with pride.

So be smart – value time above money, and consider carefully how you are going to spend today. These next twenty-four hours are a gift that must not be squandered.

As they say: today is the first day of the rest of your life.

So live it boldly.

54.
TAKE CARE OF YOUR OF YOUR POSSESSIONS

I have talked about taking care of your family and friends and your time, but how you take care of your possessions also says a lot about you.

We live in a consumer-driven world, where if something breaks, we chuck it. That is bad for the soul as well as the environment.

The investor Warren Buffett often gives this advice to those who want to replicate his success: you shouldn't buy a stock unless you'd be happy to hold on to it if the stock market shut down for ten years.

I think it's a good guide for other purchases, too. Think you might be happy to wear that coat for the next decade? Then go ahead and buy it. Think that bit of equipment is robust enough to last ten years? Then choose it over the cheaper, flimsier option.

Learn to fix things and to look after your things. It is the mark of a man.

When I meet people who are careful of and grateful for the possessions they have, I am always impressed.

55.
THE
RISK :
REWARD
RATIO

In mountaineering, climbers become very familiar with the 'risk : reward ratio'.

There are always crunch times on a mountain when you have to weigh up the odds for success against the risks of cold, bad weather or avalanche. But in essence the choice is simple – **you cannot reach the big summits if you do not accept the big risks.**

If you risk nothing, you gain nothing.

The great climbers know that great summits don't come easy – they require huge, concerted, continuous effort. But mountains reward real effort. So does life and business.

Everything that is worthwhile requires risk and effort. If it was easy, then everyone would succeed.

Having a big goal is the easy bit. The part that separates the many from the few is how willing you are to go through the pain. How able you are to hold on and to keep going when it is tough?

The French Foreign Legion, with whom I once did simulated basic training in the deserts of North Africa, describe what it takes to earn the coveted cap, the képi blanc cap: 'A thousand barrels of sweat.'

That is a lot of sweat! Trust me.

But ask any Legionnaire if it was worth it and I can tell you their answer. Every time. Because **the pain and the discomfort, the blisters and the aching muscles, don't last for ever**. But the pride in an achievement reached or dream attained will be with you for the rest of your days.

The greater the effort, the better the reward. So learn to embrace hard work and great effort and risk. Without them, there can be no meaningful achievement.

56.
TENTATIVE IS NO POWER

When I was about 15 years old, I heard an American athlete say this, 'Tentative is no power.' It took me a while to work out what he meant.

Roman commanders would often order the burning of bridges after having crossed them to prevent their own armies from fleeing in the face of danger. If a soldier tried to flee, he would eventually be backed up against the river and have to fight – or die trying to escape.

There was no going back. It was total commitment.

Dramatic, but effective.

Tentative is the opposite. It is half-hearted and timid. Tentative leaves the bridges intact – just in case. But 'just in case' gives you the option to retreat when it gets tough. And all goals – if they are big goals – get tough.

'Tentative is no power' really says that if you want something, you have to go for it – totally. All in. Heart and soul. 100 per cent.

When you totally commit to something, you force yourself to find a way, however hard – because there is no alternative. There are no bridges.

Don't believe me? Then ask a professional rugby player. If you throw yourself into that rugby tackle hard, then you win; but hit it half-heartedly and tentatively – and you get injured.

Annoying but true!

Boldness has genius, power and magic in it. It's like a secret ingredient that, when added to a tricky situation, can transform outcomes.

The wild demands boldness. When you jump off a cliff, or cross a crevasse, or wade through a raging river, you don't get many second chances. You have to get it right first time, and indecision and half-heartedness can cost you dearly.

There can be a fine line between boldness and recklessness (which is why it's often said that you get bold mountaineers and old mountaineers, but not many bold, old mountaineers!). **But boldness is not recklessness.** It is not 'winging it' without thinking through the consequences of your actions. It isn't 'not having a strategy or a back-up plan', both of which can be important parts of being bold.

It is simply, once all your options have been assessed, committing totally to that course of action, and refusing to give up in the face of adversity.

It's just another one of the universe's hidden truths. And it is one that I love because it doesn't require good A-level results or a university degree!

It is a simple principle that we can all learn, practise, and use to win where others retreat and fail.

57.
EVERY TIME YOU SURPRISE YOURSELF... YOU INSPIRE YOURSELF

SAS selection is designed to test you.

Any mental flaw, any physical failing will be exposed by the relentless series of challenges aimed at finding your breaking point. Lung-bursting cross-mountain marches through the snow, uphill sprints, carrying another recruit in a fireman's lift up and down steep hills, often in driving rain, sometimes in sub-zero temperatures.

As selection goes on, these 'beasting' sessions get harder and harder.

And yet I also found that the more of them I came through in one piece (albeit exhausted and battered), the more easily I could cope with them. **It was the SAS way of testing our mental resolve through physical battering.**

Selection is all about realizing that the pain never lasts for ever. And every time I was tested and I hung on in there, the better I understood that it was just a question of doing it again – one more time – until someone eventually said it was the end, and I had passed.

I now know that unless you really, truly test yourself, you'll never have any idea just how capable you can be. And with each small achievement, your confidence will grow.

Most people never reach their limit because they are never sufficiently tested.

This means I've got two good pieces of news for you.

The first is that whenever you do something beyond your 'comfort zone' and realize you are still standing, the more you will *believe* that the impossible is actually possible. And on the road to success, belief is everything.

And the second piece of news is that we all have much further to push ourselves than we might initially imagine. **Inside us all, just waiting to be tested, is a better, bolder, braver version of who we think we are.**

All you have to do is give it an opportunity to be unleashed.

So pick big targets and surprise yourself with how capable you really are deep down.

Remember David and Goliath? Rather than David, the young shepherd boy, looking at this giant of a warrior and thinking, 'Yikes, he's huge, I'm beat' – he thought, 'With a target that big, how can I possibly miss!'

Success, in life and adventure, is dependent on the retraining of our mind.

58.
DO NOT JUDGE SOMEONE BY THEIR STATUS

One of the best things about expeditions into the wild is that they restore a healthy perspective to our lives. It's as if nature gives our internal hard drive a giant re-boot and de-frag – shifting everything back into a correct and natural order.

I notice it not only in the big things, but also in the smaller stuff, such as what we talk about in the mountains. So often, when I take a group of people from a variety of backgrounds out into the back country, the topics of conversation change as we make progress on our journey.

At first it's the usual 'So what do you do?' or 'Where do you live?', and you can see the mental calculations going on: he's more successful than me, she's richer than me, he went to university, she's got flashier gear than me…

It's as if everyone is assessing everyone else to see where they are in this illusionary pecking order.

But after a few days or weeks, people change.

You care more if someone has been good company, has got on with their duties, has been cheerful, has pulled their weight.

On every adventure you are reminded that nobility is not a birthright.

You see, the wild levels us – we all start off equal again, our so-called status counts for nothing. **It's your attitude that determines your altitude, not your past.**

The wild forces us to live in the present, and it doesn't care about our past or future. It makes us all a little naked, a little vulnerable – it is hard to hide who we are.

And therein lies the beauty. We can't pretend for long.

What is important in life becomes the stuff that really matters on that mountain.

Such as whether someone will share their water bottle when you are thirsty, offer you their last plaster for your blisters, or carry some of your load when you are weary. These character traits elevate people.

I often say that our lives can all too easily become 'fluffy' – and what I mean is that so often the trivial gets revered.

But the wild is much more raw, and the fluff that we all carry matters less – it is as if the fluff gets blown away.

Remember that society's status is hollow and transitory, but genuine character and action endures and shines long after the fluff has gone.

So seek genuine character in yourself and gravitate towards it in others. And if you find yourself (as we all do occasionally) being too impressed by the hollow masters such as status, power, fame or money, take a trip to the wild with some friends, and remind yourself that the most precious things in life cost the least.

59.
CREATURE COMFORTS ARE ONLY TEMPORARY

It was one of the most painful lessons of my life.

It was during the first time I attempted SAS selection. I was totally lost in a vast boggy wetland, torrential rain was driving down, and I was utterly spent.

I was also way behind time, and I knew it.

When I finally made it to the penultimate checkpoint, the corporals kept me there doing endless press-ups in the wet marsh with my heavy pack still on my back. I knew this was costing me even more valuable time and energy.

I was feeling fainter and fainter; I knew things were bad.

I was soon off again, wading across a fast-flowing, waist-deep stream, before climbing up through knee-deep mud towards the next 2,000-foot (600-metre) mountain ridge-line. I just had to keep going. Ten miles. Twenty miles. 'Nothing good comes from quitting,' I told myself, over and over again. 'If I keep going, I will pass.'

But I was getting more and more delirious with fatigue. I didn't know why this was happening, and I couldn't control it. Maybe I hadn't eaten or drunk enough, or perhaps it was just that the months of this relentless pace were finally taking their toll and I was at my limit.

Every couple of paces, my knees would buckle. If I stumbled, I couldn't stop myself from falling.

Eventually I saw the trucks in the distance below me, symbolizing the end point. Wisps of smoke from army Hexi stoves curled upwards from the woods. Soon I would be warm, soon I would have a cup of hot tea. It was all I wanted.

But when I reached the end checkpoint I was told I had been failed – I had been too slow. My world fell inwards. I was sent off to make camp in the woods and rest for the night. The remaining recruits would be heading out for the night march in a few hours.

The next morning I would be returned to camp with the others who hadn't made the grade. I was totally dejected.

That night in those woods, warm and dry under my shelter, blisters attended to, dry socks on, and out of the wind and rain, I learnt an enduring lesson: warm and dry doesn't mean fulfilled and happy.

Only a few hours earlier I had been longing to be warm and dry and safe. Yet lying there, knowing that my buddies were starting out on a gruelling night march without me, was pure agony. Never has anyone wanted to be cold, wet and tired as much as I did right then. And never have the comforts of shelter and food meant so little to me.

You see, being dry and warm in life, but with no purpose, is no consolation for being in the heat of the arena in pursuit of your goals.

Don't get me wrong, warm and dry is great as a reward 'afterwards', and we should all regularly enjoy some time chilling, doing 'nothing' – but if all you do is 'nothing', you will find it a very hollow existence.

(So yes, I went back on the next Selection course and went through those 11 months of SAS hell again – and I passed. I was cold, wet and exhausted throughout, so that now, when I relax, I feel that huge sense of pride for having endured.)

Once you commit to your goal, don't get swayed by the temporary lure of creature comforts and easy feelings – instead, keep focused, and remember the pain never lasts for ever, but the pride in having followed your calling will.

60.
DON'T DWELL ON MISTAKES

Mistakes are for learning from, not dwelling on. If you muck something up, spend a few minutes working out why, learn the lesson, then move swiftly on.

Dwelling on mistakes, endlessly replaying scenes in your head, only makes them grow.

So the next time you find yourself lying in bed at night, cursing your stupidity or foolishness, it's worth reminding yourself that, in all probability, the mistake isn't that big a deal to anyone else. Too often we can be our own harshest critic and worst enemy. Let it go and don't waste more energy on regrets than you need to.

Look objectively. Learn humbly. Smile positively. Then move on, wiser and smarter than before.

There's a very good reason why you made a mistake: you're human! We all make them from time to time. Which is why we should also be understanding and forgiving when someone else makes one.

Ever heard the phrase 'When you're in a hole, stop digging'? It's the same with mistakes. **Don't give the mistake more power than it warrants by squandering precious time worrying about it.**

Yesterday is not ours to recover, but tomorrow is ours to win or lose.

Oh, and if you want to be really smart, then learn from the mistakes that other people make, so as to avoid the pain yourself.
(A newspaper is a good place to start, and it is one of the few benefits of reading them!)

61.
GET OUT OF YOUR COMFORT PIT

The thing about a 'comfort zone' is that it sounds, well, just too comfortable – and when you are too comfortable you lose your edge. That's why I call it a comfort *pit*, because a pit is somewhere you want to get out of as fast as possible.

Pits are not good places to live in, if you want to soar like the eagles.

The longer we spend in one place doing the same things over and over, the more of life we are missing out on – and the harder it becomes to change our ways. Like water running over rock, you start to gouge out a little groove for yourself. Over the years, that groove then becomes a deep gorge, and it becomes harder and harder to change its course.

It takes guts to get out of the ruts, but when you decide to try something new or attempt something bold and ambitious, the rewards are yours for the reaping. You start to feel alive. You start to notice the possibilities all around. And you get that thrill of discovery as you remind yourself you are capable of doing so much more.

People get nervous when they try new things, yet the definition of madness is doing the same thing over and over and expecting a different result.

The trick is not to let those nervous feelings stop you from going for your 'impossible'.

It's totally normal to feel a bit fearful, shaky and unsure. I feel those feelings often before a big climb or before dropping into a harsh jungle. **But butterflies in your stomach don't mean that you should keep things as they are: they are the tell-tale signs that an adventure is about to begin!**

So whenever you feel too comfortable, look around you, raise your eyes, and get climbing before the pit becomes too deep.

To reach great heights will always require us to feel a healthy amount of trepidation. Get used to it. It is a feeling that all champions must learn to embrace.

62.
TWO EARS, ONE MOUTH

My mum and dad often told me that I had two ears and one mouth and that I should use them in that proportion. It is good advice.

If you're always thinking about what you want to say, then you're never really listening to what other people are saying. And that means you are missing out.

In a survival situation, if you talk more than you listen, you risk missing some vital piece of knowledge, whether it is the sound of a predator's warning or a distant river that could save your life.

Likewise in life, if you talk too much, you'll miss the chance to get to know other people properly and understand their points of view fully.

Conversely, if you make sure the listening exceeds the talking, then when you do speak, you'll find that people will be far more interested in what you have to say. Firstly because they'll assume what you're saying is considered and of value, and secondly they won't be sick of the sound of your voice!

People always value others who really listen to them. Quiet, considered and genuine listening is such a gift to give someone, and you will become recognized and loved for this skill.

It is always empowering to others if you truly listen well.

And don't listen to reply, but listen to understand. That means don't always be thinking of your next sentence or your reply while people are talking – rather just listen carefully to understand how they are feeling or what they are imparting.

It sounds simple but so few people do this, and it is a big part of why many never reach their full potential in life.

You know the expression: empty vessels make the most noise. It is true. The best adventurers and climbers, and the most successful people I know in life, are all great listeners, and they don't talk too much. They want to weigh every option carefully, and they take time to absorb the information coming at them.

It is all too easy not to listen properly and to jump into a perspective or decision without considering the implications – but if you listen diligently, it gives you precious time to assess a situation properly.

This has saved my life many times, especially when I have received detailed safety briefings from local rangers before entering the wild. Listen carefully – your life might depend on others' experience and advice.

So make sure you use your ears and your mouth in the correct ratio – and listen twice as much as you talk. It is a firm habit of successful people.

63.
LET OTHERS SHINE

We have all met them – the people who, after you've recounted some fun story where maybe you caught a fish or fell off your bicycle, go on to tell an even funnier story about a bigger fish or a higher speed wipe-out!

And it makes you feel pretty small.

We all have bigger and better stories, but it's a good quality to be able to hold your tongue and allow the storyteller their moment in the sun.

No one likes a boaster – no matter how big their fish is or how dramatic the fall. I, for one, much prefer the company of people who let others shine, who listen to their stories and don't feel the need to be better/faster/funnier/louder.

Always remember that when someone is telling you a story, it's probably because it's about something that is important to them. You wouldn't go trampling over their possessions, so don't go trampling over their achievements either.

Everyone will warm to you when you sit back and enjoy their stories. And remember: you don't want to end up successful but without buddies!

64.
LEAD
BY
EXAMPLE

Let me introduce you to the secret of good leadership (and it's not about being loud and bossy!). Good leadership is all about caring for people, and inspiring people to be the best they can.

The story of Ernest Shackleton, the polar explorer, is often cited as one of the great epics of human survival, but it is also one of the best examples of the difference good leadership can make.

In 1914 he sailed to the South Atlantic with the aim of exploring new territory in Antarctica. In January 1915, about 100 miles north of Antarctica, his boat, the *Endurance*, became trapped in the polar ice floes.

His men tried to break the ice with picks but it was too thick. The only thing to do was to wait for the weather to change and the ice to melt.

Everyone on board knew they were in for a long wait.

In sub-zero temperatures, with no radio and no means of contacting the rest of the world, it would have been quite understandable if the men on Shackleton's boat descended into madness and violence.

Yet Shackleton knew how to look after his men. He kept them busy and valued – whether it was catching seals for meat and blubber, or organizing scientific research or challenging mental and physical games.

Shackleton also knew that his men's survival would be based on their ability to hold on to hope. He did more than his regular share of the chores and he never let the conversation hint at anything other than a successful return home.

Perpetual darkness, the unknown, freezing temperatures and endless waiting can be terrifying conditions to endure, piling pressure on to the mental resolve of every man on board. Shackleton knew that depression and resentment were a greater threat to survival than hypothermia, so he did all he could to counter negative emotions.

When spring came, the movement of the melting ice did not free the *Endurance* as had been hoped. Instead the ice started to shatter their one chance of salvation, beam by beam. Their precious ship was being steadily crushed by the awesome power of the pack ice.

After weeks of this groaning, creaking ice – during which the frozen sea had torn apart the giant oak timbers of the *Endurance* as if they were matchsticks – an ominous silence descended across the vast, white, ice desert, and the remains of their ship slipped beneath the waves.

The men were staring down the barrel of a lingering death from hypothermia and starvation – any other fate seemed impossible.

How does a great leader respond to that sort of catastrophe?

He gave them hope and purpose, and ingrained in them a determination to hold fast and to look after each other. He told them that their survival would come down to maintaining a positive attitude – however hard the journey ahead would become.

Above all, he was determined not to lose one single man.

For the next six months, Shackleton's men camped on an ice floe in the hope it would drift towards land. When it did not, they finally took to dragging the *Endurance*'s heavy lifeboats towards open water. Inch by inch.

They then spent five harrowing days at sea, like specks of dust in a giant ice cooler, before finally landing on Elephant Island – freezing cold and soaked to the skin by the icy water. They might have been on solid land, but they were still in one of the most treacherous, barren places on Earth, with dwindling supplies and strength – and no chance of rescue.

Their last remaining option was to send out a small team in one of the lifeboats with the goal of reaching South Georgia, a whaling station about a month's sail to the north.

Everyone knew that the likelihood of navigating, and surviving, across one of the wildest stretches of icy ocean, in just a tiny open boat, was slim in the extreme.

Shackleton could have sent someone else on that most treacherous of missions, but he knew he had to lead that small team himself.

What then followed was one of the greatest journeys of hardship, skill, endurance and courage before they finally made it to the wild, mountainous coastline of South Georgia.

But even when he landed, the men then had to cross, on foot, a huge, uncharted, windswept mountain range, before descending through mile after mile of treacherous ice and crevasses, finally to reach the distant inhabited part of the island.

From South Georgia, Shackleton then made no less than four rescue attempts to reach those left on Elephant Island. He refused to give up.

Finally, after two years in the harshest conditions known to man, with only the most basic of equipment (no GPS or Gore-tex back then, remember), every single one of Shackleton's men were rescued.

Many other expeditions have had better supplies, better back-up, better communications – but they did not have Shackleton's leadership.

The power of great leadership is beyond measure, and the heart of all great leadership is found in leading by example. Example in terms of your ethics, your faith, your care and your courage.

There is immense power in learning these core leadership lessons – vision, example and care.

65.
FUEL WELL, TRAIN REGULARLY

I have talked a lot in this book about attitudes of the mind being the key to success, but there is one other factor that can't be overlooked. Without the right long-term fuel and training, you will dramatically reduce your ability to reach your goals.

If you have a great Ferrari and pour old tractor diesel into it, you are unlikely to get anything out of it except stinking black smoke and a lot of backfiring!

Our bodies are the same. However good our physical frame, if we don't fuel and train it properly, it will under-perform (and over-belch).

Don't think you can live off processed food, never train your body physically, and still go on to climb your own personal Everest.

The good news is that keeping your body in shape isn't rocket science.

First up, nutrition in a nutshell: avoid, as much as you possibly can: processed food, white sugar, too much salt, saturated fat, white bread, white flour, and too much booze.

Instead, eat lots of fruit and vegetables, and eat them raw whenever you can. Eat whole grains, like brown rice and brown bread, and choose foods that are found in nature – you don't get many doughnuts hanging on trees! Aim to eat natural fats such as nuts and avocados, and seek out the lean proteins of turkey and fish rather than beef and pork.

If you do this, you will shed weight and power your muscles, brain and heart.

I like to follow the 80:20 rule. Eat healthily for 80 per cent of the time, and then you can have a treat for the remaining 20 per cent of the time.

(By the way, if you become obsessive about healthy eating, then life can be pretty dull; likewise, if all you do is gorge on chocolate, then the enjoyment will go out of chocolate.) So have treats, but make them treats rather than staples. And for every bad thing you eat, try to double up on the good. Moderation is key.

That's how I try to fuel my body.

Now on to physical training.

The key to keeping fit is to make exercise a habit and make everyday jobs into exercise.

My routine means I train five or six days a week. But you can do less. Three times a week is fine. I make sure to mix it up to include cardio, strength and flexibility, and often all at the same time.

As for duration of exercise: less is so often more. I prefer to train really hard at a high intensity for 30–40 minutes rather than to go steady for an hour. The higher intensity stimulates your metabolism for longer and promotes greater muscle regrowth.

The other key is to make exercise fun – find the thing you enjoy, whether it is tennis, hiking or circuit-training with a partner. When training is fun, it is always easier. The time flies by.

And remember that there is always an excuse not to exercise. 'My training buddy is ill.' 'I'm on holiday.' 'I'm travelling this week.' But don't listen to that 'lazy-you' on your shoulder. I do yoga in an airport, pull-ups in the jungle, even stair sprints in a hotel. You can get your heart rate high wherever you are.

Even if you have no time for a few days in a row, doing a high-intensity circuit of bodyweight exercises for two or three minutes can massively improve your fitness and alter your mood for the better.

The final part of a healthy lifestyle is to make exercise part of how you live your life.

By this I mean run up the stairs rather than take the lift, or climb up the escalators rather than stand still – whatever it is, do it with vigour and energy, and you will live to be a hundred.

(Actually, that bit I can't guarantee, but I can promise you that you'll live a fitter, more fulfilled life, as making exercise part of your everyday routine stimulates blood flow and releases good endorphins – both of which help to keep all your systems working to the best of their ability.)

So there we go: eat healthy, and exercise smart. Nicely compiled into one easy chapter. I told you it wasn't rocket science.

66.
THE WILL TO WIN MEANS NOTHING WITHOUT THE WILL TO TRAIN

I have met a lot of people over the years who professed that they would do whatever it took to win a race or climb a big mountain. But sometimes the will to win just isn't enough.

In fact, the will to win means nothing if you don't also have the will to train.

The day of the race is the easy bit: all eyes are on you and the adrenalin is running high. **But the race or the battle is really won or lost in the build-up:** the unglamorous times when it is raining at 5.30 a.m. and you don't want to get out of your warm bed to go for a run.

So, don't fall into the trap of trying hard but lacking the skills or resources that you can only gain through training.

I love the story of Daley Thompson, the decathlete who won gold at two Olympics.

He used to say his favourite day of the year to train was Christmas Day, as he knew it would be the only day his competitors wouldn't be training. That is commitment, and it is part of why he won – he saw it as a chance to get 1/365th quicker than his rivals!

So, remember that our goals are reached by how we prepare and train in the many months before crunch time. Train right, and the summit or gold medal will be the inevitable culmination of your commitment.

I like that, because it means the rewards go to the dogged rather than the brilliant.

67.
GIVE IT AWAY!

Now that you are working hard and smart, you might find you start earning well. Not always, but often, when people love what they do and work with incredibly good ethics and determination, financial success follows.

This chapter is about making sure that, if you go on to do well financially, you are properly equipped to deal with it – so that you always control the money, rather than the money controlling you.

Throughout this book, I've encouraged you to be generous with your time, your talents and your spirit. The reason for this is simple: being generous is a key trait of happiness.

And without happiness, can we really claim to be successful?

But a part of your success should also be to make sure you are generous with your money.

I'm going to show you how giving away part of our hard-earned money is fundamental to making sure we stay happy.

Clinging on too tight to belongings, talent or resources only drains people of joy. We have to keep giving in order to experience the best of life.

Now, I know that money is always a sensitive subject, and I am not going to tell you that there is only one way to give your money or what percentage to give or what charities are best.

I'm going to trust that if you are smart enough to build a successful life then you should be smart enough to understand that giving money is as much about the spirit as it is about the actual amounts.

(And remember: one thing is for certain, giving money doesn't get us to Heaven. Heaven is a gift that was bought for us at a price greater than any of us can afford. But giving money away is a definite by-product of having received that gift!)

When we receive something amazing, our instinct is to want to give something in gratitude. It is how we work – so follow those natural rhythms.

Regardless of how you decide to give and how much, just ensure that giving part of your earnings to those in real need becomes a joyful part of your life.

Give to friends who do amazing jobs but who earn very little, give to charities that move you, give to those the world overlooks, give as your heart tells you – and learn to listen to it.

And by all means live a great life yourself along the way – why not? You have worked hard for it, paid your taxes and you deserve it. The main thing to remember, though, is to keep giving lots of money away as well.

If you do, then, in return, it will do many things for you…

This attitude will ensure that money never makes a slave of you – it will keep you in control of it, rather than it controlling you.

It will ensure that you treat money as a resource given to you to allow you to improve your life and those you have the power to touch around you. Always use it accordingly.

It will ensure you keep light fingers with regard to money matters – which means that you don't care too much about holding on to it, and you can let it pass through your hands easily to those in more need.

Remember: the process of giving will always benefit you more than the extra funds themselves ever can.

There is a powerful parable in the Gospels of Mark and John, where Jesus and his disciples watch the people arrive at the temple and make their donations. Many make a big show of offering large sums, a spectacle for all to admire.

But then an old widow quietly offers two of the smallest coins in circulation at that time, called mites.

Jesus explains to his followers that the widow's contribution of two mites, though small in financial terms, means more to God than the larger donations.

The parable reminds us that it isn't about the amount, it's about the spirit.

The old widow got it right, and the real legacy of her giving has endured far beyond any amount of money ever could.

So build for eternity, not for the temporary – and always give with this in mind.

68.
CHEERFULNESS IN ADVERSITY

The Royal Marine Commandos, with whom I worked a lot in my military days, have the phrase 'Cheerfulness in Adversity' as one of their founding principles – and it is a great one to live by.

It is easy to be cheerful when everything is going like a song, but the real time to be cheerful is when everything is going dead wrong!

I remember in the North African desert once, when we were training with the French Foreign Legionnaires, that we had a particularly unpleasant night. The corporals took shifts to ensure that we were woken up every 15 minutes until dawn.

They would burst in and throw our kit all around and out of the windows, turn the beds upside down, empty the lockers into the desert sand, only to do it all over again as soon as we had tidied up. It was a real ball-breaker of a night.

But I will never forget one of the recruits, Bobby. At 4.30 a.m., during our darkest, most exhausting hour, when the corporals were in full swing and we had been up all night in the face of this mindless, sleep-defying beasting, Bobby looked at us, smiled and said: 'Breakfast is comin'!'

There was something about the way he said it, with a wry grin as he set about retrieving his pile of kit from the rafters of the barrack block, that lifted all our spirits like nothing you could imagine.

From then on, whenever something has got really tough, I say to myself: 'Don't worry – breakfast is comin'!' And it always makes me smile.

You see, Bobby knew that when it gets hard we all have two responses to choose from: to moan, or to put our heads down, smile and get on with it.

Remember: no one likes a moaner.

Wouldn't we all rather work with someone who, when the workload gets insane, simply says: 'Right, let's put some music on, divide up the tasks and get cracking. Breakfast is comin'!'

Life is full of rough patches. All big goals, however glamorous on paper, will inevitably involve a load of boring tasks along the way – it's just the way things are.

Moaning and being miserable doesn't change the facts – nor does it improve the situation. In fact, it makes a bad situation worse.

When I'm on expeditions, I value cheerfulness almost as much as fresh water. And when you're in life-and-death situations, it's priceless.

You can't always choose your situation, but you can always choose your attitude.

Not only can positive thinking lead to positive outcomes, but there's another very good reason why cheerfulness is good for survival: people are more likely to want to help you and stick with you.

And in adversity, you're going to want all the help you can get.

So learn from the Commandos, smile when it is raining, and show cheerfulness in adversity – and look at the hard times as chances to show your mettle.

'Breakfast is comin'!'

69.
WHEN YOU'RE GOING THROUGH THROUGH HELL, KEEP GOING

Whether I have been in the middle of a dusty, barren desert, stuck in a mosquito-infested swamp, or freezing cold and wet in the middle of the ocean, there is always one thing I tell myself above everything else (and it is an easy one to remember, even when you are dog tired and not feeling particularly brave or strong). It's this…

…just keep going. JKG.

Winston Churchill said it in one of the darkest moments of World War Two, when the outlook was as bleak as it had ever been. On 10 May 1940, the British looked to be finished. They stood alone against the vicious and victorious Nazis.

Two weeks after Churchill came to power, France was knocked out of the war, and 340,000 British troops had to scramble to escape over the beaches at Dunkirk. The Germans had absolute control of all of Europe.

It seemed impossible that Britain could survive.

What was Churchill's response? 'When you're going through hell, keep going.'

It is reassuring to know that the real heart of survival is as simple as this. All you have to do is to keep putting one foot in front of the other. Even if you don't make much progress, you just have to keep going. It is not only the heart of survival, it is also the key to success.

It's really not that different when we face traumas elsewhere in our lives. Bereavement, illness and heartbreak are part of every human life. Sometimes the emotional impact of these events can bring us to our knees. But the way through is always the same: keep going.

When we give up, we know our destiny. When we keep going, we earn the right to choose our fate.

Ingrain it in your DNA: JKG.

70.
SOMETIMES AN EMBER IS ALL YOU NEED

In the wild, an ember, a single spark, can save your life. And it can change your life, too.

Take the story of Beck Weathers, the high-altitude mountaineer left for dead on Everest.

On the morning of 10 May 1996, as Beck made his final ascent towards the summit, he was struck by an extreme case of snow-blindness. With no way of seeing where he was going, he could do nothing but hunker down and hope for rescue.

Storm clouds began to roll across the peak, and in minutes he found himself in the middle of a raging blizzard. Seventy-mile-an-hour winds and driven snow blasted the side of the mountain, hitting Beck with a wind chill of 100° below zero.

Finally, some climbers returning from the summit stumbled upon Beck and attempted to help him down the mountain. They did their best, despite whiteout conditions, but eventually the gale-force winds, lack of oxygen and unrelenting storm forced the climbers to stop and huddle together for warmth.

When there was finally a lull in the storm, one of the climbers, Mike Groom, knew he had a small window in which to go for help. He left Weathers and four other climbers, all of whom were nearly unconscious, to return to the high camp to get help.

Help arrived a few hours later. Three of the climbers were led back to camp, but Beck and one other climber had both fallen into a hypothermic coma and were unresponsive.

The rescuers decided that nothing could be done to save these people – the conditions were too dangerous to drag their unconscious bodies – and they were left for dead on the side of the mountain.

All night Beck lay on his back, slowly freezing to death in the bitter cold. Though he was lying only 300 yards from camp, at that altitude the distance might as well have been 300 miles. Frostbite set in on his nose and both of his hands.

Here would be his final resting place, buried under the snow and exposed to extreme cold, ice and wind.

The next morning, two others returned to the two stricken climbers' position. After chipping blocks of ice off their faces, they reported them to be breathing, but severely frostbitten and 'as close to death as a human being can be'.

The call once again was made to leave them for dead. The climbers trudged back to camp and reported the deaths.

But then something incredible happened. Beck Weathers opened his eyes.

Beck says he saw his wife and kids standing in front of him, calling out to him.

This was the ember.

He slowly dragged himself to his feet and started stumbling forward.

He was completely blind in one eye, which was frozen shut by the cold, and had a visibility range of barely two feet in the other eye. His entire body was like ice, and he was crippled by altitude sickness. Yet he kept stumbling on.

Finally, against all odds, Beck Weathers lurched into camp.

Beck lost both his hands and his nose to frostbite, yet that tiny ember that burnt within him, that ember of hope from his family, was all he needed to get up and to move.

That ember saved his life.

Never underestimate the human spirit.

Within us all are incredible embers of dreams, hopes and aspirations, waiting for us to breathe them into life.

And it only takes a tiny ember to start a great fire.

71.
HOW YOU SPEAK ABOUT OTHERS SPEAKS LOUDEST ABOUT YOURSELF

Here is a great definition of gossip I once heard: 'If the person you're speaking to will think worse or less of the person you're speaking about, then it's gossip, so cut it out!'

But wow, how people love to gossip (and we are all guilty of it at times), despite the damage it causes.

The problem with gossip is that it is always at someone else's expense, however subtle the dig.

You might think you're having an idle bit of banter about someone's choice of fashion, partner or holiday, but behind the words a judgement is being made. And if that judgement is cruel, it says far more about the person doing the talking than the person being talked about.

It is so true that how people talk about others reveals most about themselves. The person who fixates on other people's appearances is so often the vainest person, underneath all the bravado. The person who criticizes others' relationships usually has a load of mess in their own. And the person who is constantly talking about how much or little other people earn is most likely the chippy one that feels the world owes them a living.

By putting others down, people hope it might elevate themselves. But it actually does the opposite. Friends might pretend they find your comments funny, but in the long term people will be wary of you. And of course they will think: 'Well, if he can say that about someone else, he can say it about me, too.'

So, instead, be the sort of person who is known never to speak ill of others. And people will love you for it. It is that rare.

And remember: when you seek the good in people, you almost always find it.

Oh, and if you keep speaking good of people, then over time you will find *yourself* becoming more optimistic and positive.

That's part of the reward.

72.
GRATITUDE, GRATITUDE, GRATITUDE

Being grateful is one of the best natural combatants against depression I know – and I just can't seem to figure out why or how it works!

But it does, and that's what matters. **Being thankful almost always makes you feel better.**

Now, sometimes we get down, especially when life gets rough. But how we respond determines our future. If we get angry or bitter or cynical, guess what? We attract more of that negative stuff into our lives. But if we respond with gratitude for the many simple blessings we have – whether it is our health, family, friends, or even just our life – somehow it keeps some perspective on the tough stuff and makes our world a better place.

That's why, as a family, we always try to say Grace before meals – it is good for us all to remember the bigger picture sometimes. It is a moment when we can stop the hurry through the day and give a few seconds just to say thank you. Sounds old-fashioned? Well, maybe Grandma knows best.

By the way, sometimes it can be a little embarrassing saying Grace when we have friends round – but I have found that people tend to love it, even if it is not something they do themselves. It somehow makes for good vibes round a table. It means we step out of our own bubble of 'stuff' and think of and appreciate other people.

You don't have to have a faith to benefit from the positive effects of gratitude – it is just another of those great laws of the universe. When you are grateful, you often end up smiling.

Another big part of gratitude is not taking good things in our lives for granted. **Complacency can be one of the biggest killers in the wild – I have seen this first hand all too often – and it is the same in life.**

Whether it is the wife, husband, girlfriend, boyfriend, family or friends, so often those closest to us are the ones who get the *worst* of us. It is as if we feel that they are the only ones we can be grumpy with, and we save our best for our guests or for work. But this is a recipe for struggle.

The smart man and woman save the best for those they love.

If we show our loved ones the most gratitude every day, then life will smile on us in return.

Gratitude, gratitude, gratitude: three words to help you thrive. Trust me.

73.
WHEN LIFE HANDS YOU A LEMON, MAKE LEMONADE

This always makes me chuckle. But the ability to turn sour, unwanted lemons into sweet, sparkling lemonade is one of the key traits of successful people, and it just takes a little bit of imagination and lots of hard work.

Without doubt, we all get handed 'lemons' sometimes in life. No one is immune from this. Maybe it's an incurable illness, or a soldier caught in a roadside bomb; maybe it's a duff education, a dysfunctional upbringing, or perhaps your plane crashes in the jungle, your car breaks down in the desert or you lose a loved one.

Bad things happen. We all know that, right?

But how we respond is where our future lies.

One of the best survival techniques is ingenuity: using the mundane to create the brilliant. It might be as simple as putting your sock over your boot to enable you to cross the slippery ice on a glacier, or working out how to cross a ravine by improvising a grappling hook from an old rope and an animal trap.

It is all about thinking smart, thinking differently – thinking left-field.

Necessity is the mother of invention – meaning if you don't have the thing you need, then you simply have to invent something that will do the job using what you do have, however long it takes or hard it might be. And nothing teaches you to invent and improvise like adventure: you have to use what you've got to make whatever you can.

Surviving in the wild stretches us – it is part of the magic. But when you embrace that challenge, then the journey out of there begins.

Likewise, when we take what life has given us, however small a seed, and we determine to make something of it through hard work, imagination and resourcefulness, we can begin to break the mould.

You might think that successful people were given all the raw resources on a plate – as if the ingredients were just lying around waiting to be picked up. But life isn't like that.

Even with those lucky people who have had the best education, the best clothes, food and shoes growing up, it doesn't guarantee anything. It might give them some more opportunities, but unless you get out there, grab those opportunities and work them, they mean nothing.

Successful people take what they have around them, however meagre, and they make something of it. It might be small at first, but it is a step forward, a rung on the ladder, and it is this positive step that leads them on.

Look at the stories of people who have changed the world – they have so often started with little, but they distinguished themselves by how they approached life, opportunity, relationships and struggle. Martin Luther King, Nelson Mandela, Gandhi. You name them. The list is huge but the common qualities are small.

Resourcefulness and a determination to survive the 'lemons' are invariably at the heart of these successes.

The secret to a life well lived is taking the resources around us – the people we know, the possessions we own, the skills we've acquired – and combining them in such a way that they add up to something greater than their constituent parts.

That's the lemonade bit.

So often in the wild I have felt totally beaten, but I have kept going, kept trying to think smart, be resourceful, positive, energetic – despite the fatigue – and it has always made a critical difference.

We can't always choose our circumstances but we can choose how we respond to what life throws at us, and there is power when we realize our ability to alter our destiny.

A life in the wild has taught me not to fear the unexpected, but to embrace it. In fact, I have learnt that those curve balls from left-field are very often the making of us.

74.
CRISIS
=
DANGER
+
OPPORTUNITY

President John F. Kennedy once gave a speech where he said that when written in Chinese the word 'crisis' was formed from two characters – one represents danger, the other represents opportunity.

It's a great perspective, because so often we see a crisis as something to be avoided, when in reality it can conceal both adventure and advantage.

I am not saying we should seek out a drama, but rather, when crisis strikes, we should use it.

Opportunity will be hidden among the chaos.

Storms clean the oceans, winds carry the seeds.

I once asked one of the most successful people I know what the key to his success had been. He said it was very clear. Every deal had a crunch time, a moment when the whole venture was held in the balance. It was in these times that he came alive, and he always delivered.

In short, he knew he was great in a crisis – and the results were always huge.

Most people crumble when squeezed, but the champion feeds off it.

If I had to pick just one great trait to have in the wild, it would be this: calm in the storm.

Develop this trait, even if you don't feel it naturally applies to you. Embrace the dramas whenever you can – in order to practise!

Tell yourself: 'I am good in the crisis, I am calm in the storm.' Tell yourself this until it becomes your reality.

75.
LIGHT CAN ONLY SHINE THROUGH BROKEN VESSELS

I want the last chapter of this book to be about humanity and humility.

In order to thrive and survive in the game of life, it is important to understand that we don't have to have all parts of our life totally together – nicely sealed and wrapped – for it to be a success.

In fact, the opposite is true.

To live a life of adventure and impact we just need to have the will, and then to begin. There is power in that first simple step. The rest is then the process – hard and challenging, to be sure – but still a process. We are limited only by the extent of our courage, tenacity and vision.

We can all push the boundaries, make a difference, empower, encourage, and better many lives.

None of this requires us to be perfect and sorted first.

Life is a journey and we are all learning every day. Embrace that. Growing pains are part of life!

And finally, remember that light can only shine through broken vessels, and we are all a little broken. **Sometimes it is the broken-ness that gives us the fire.**

But it is when we know our need to change that we can finally begin to grow.

Here's to your own great adventure...

Born Survivor

Bear Grylls

Bear Grylls is no stranger to extremes. Trained by the British SAS to stay alive in some of the most inhospitable places on earth, in 1996 he suffered a horrendous parachuting accident that left his back broken in three places. Despite this, after months of rehabilitation, he followed his childhood dream and became the youngest Briton ever to reach the summit of Everest and survive.

Now, in *Born Survivor*, Bear shows us how, armed with the correct know-how and a determination to stay alive, all of us have the potential to beat the elements in even the bleakest of situations. From crossing piranha-infested rivers and killing deadly snakes to finding water in even the harshest deserts and fighting off grizzly bears – all manner of survival techniques from our most dangerous environments are covered.

So, whether you find yourself stranded on a high mountain, marooned on a desert island, abandoned in a rainforest or lost in the snowy outbacks of Alaska, once you've read this book, you too will be able to tackle the wilderness . . . and survive.

Great Outdoor Adventures

Bear Grylls

Do you long for adventure without being quite sure how to find it?

Do you want to sleep under the stars and experience the wonders of the natural world?

More of us than ever are spending weekends and holidays climbing mountains, surfing waves or simply walking in the wilderness, as well as indulging in many other more extreme activities. But how can we use our time out in the open to the full?

Now, Bear Grylls, one of the most intrepid survival adventurers of our day, shares his years of experience of the world's most extreme terrain to help you get the most from the great outdoors.

So, if you've always been intrigued by kite surfing, now's the time to learn how to do it! Find out how to make a tree house, or what dangers to watch out for when you're skiing or paragliding. And if you're planning a hike, discover how to navigate across the hills without ever getting lost and what to pack in your rucksack to keep you safe.

Whether you're a novice mountaineer looking to graduate from the climbing wall to real rocks, or a weekend camper in search of a little more adventure, this is the book for you.

Living Wild

Bear Grylls

In this essential guide to living wild, Bear Grylls reveals the secrets of his years of fieldcraft experience. This is the information you *really* need to know about living in the field from the man who has passed 21 SAS selection, climbed Everest and survived in some of the most inhospitable regions on Earth. In his inimitable style, Bear has thrown out everything that's boring about scouting and fieldcraft and concentrated only on what's exciting, inspirational and a little bit edgy. Learn about:

- Hidden Dangers – the pitfalls that the seasoned field professional would know to avoid, because danger rarely announces its presence.

- Bear's Secret Scouting Tips – advice that only someone who has spent extended periods of time living in the wild can offer – lessons learnt the hard way!

- Training Exercises – ways to get your skills up to scratch before going into the field.

- Improvising in the Field – what to do when you don't have the right tools with you – necessity is the mother of all invention!

- Real-life Campfire Stories – tales from Special Forces soldiers and past and present explorers, which illustrate the importance of learning from others' mistakes and good fortunes!

It's all here, from mastering the art of making the perfect campfire and constructing the best camp, to navigating safely through all terrains in all weathers – with or without a map . . . The only other thing you'll need is this book!

Mud, Sweat and Tears
The Autobiography

Bear Grylls

Bear Grylls is a man who has always sought the ultimate in adventure. Growing up on the Isle of Wight, he was taught by his father to sail and climb at an early age. As a teenager, he found identity and purpose through both mountaineering and martial arts, which led the young adventurer to the foothills of the mighty Himalayas and a grandmaster's karate training camp in Japan.

On returning home, he embarked upon the notoriously gruelling selection course for the British Special Forces to join 21 SAS – a journey that was to push him to the very limits of physical and mental endurance.

Then, in a horrific free-fall parachuting accident in Africa, Bear broke his back in three places. It was touch and go whether he would ever walk again. However, only eighteen months later and defying doctors' expectations, Bear became one of the youngest ever climbers to scale Everest, aged only twenty-three.

But this was just the beginning of his many extraordinary adventures . . .

Known and admired by millions – whether from his global adventure TV series, as a bestselling author, or as Chief Scout to the Scouting Association – Bear Grylls has survived where few would dare to go.

Now, for the first time, Bear tells the story of his action-packed life. Gripping, moving and wildly exhilarating, *Mud, Sweat and Tears* is a must-read for adrenalin junkies and armchair adventurers alike.